THE COMING
FINANCIAL
REVOLUTION

THE COMING
FINANCIAL
REVOLUTION

God's Prophetic Plan and Purpose to Prosper His People!

BUCK STEPHENS

Destiny Image® **Publishers, Inc.**
P.O. Box 310
Shippensburg, PA 17257-0310

*"Speaking to the Purposes of God for This Generation
and for the Generations to Come"*

ISBN 0-7684-2300-7

For Worldwide Distribution
Printed in the U.S.A.

This book and all other Destiny Image, Revival Press, MercyPlace, Fresh Bread, Destiny Image Fiction, and Treasure House books are available at Christian bookstores and distributors worldwide.

1 2 3 4 5 6 7 8 / 09 08 07 06 05

For a U.S. bookstore nearest you, call
1-800-722-6774.

For more information on foreign distributors, call
717-532-3040.

Or reach us on the Internet:
www.destinyimage.com

In Loving Memory of

Larry Burkett
1939 – 2003
A True Son and Leader of
The Revolution

and

Evelyn Roberts
1917 – 2005
The Gracious First Lady
of Seed Faith Living and Giving

The seeds you both have planted are growing into
a mighty revolution! We continue to fight on
while you look on! (Hebrews 12:1)

ACKNOWLEDGMENTS

There are many who either indirectly or directly contributed to this book and to whom I wish to express my gratitude.

To my precious family. **My lovely wife, Andrea** ("Andy"), who has stood by me for 30 years in life and ministry. Your life shows the love of Christ and your godliness is an inspiration. You endured hours of my back during the writing of this book and your input and additions are part of this work. Thank you for your partnership in ministry, your love, your support, and your tenacious commitment to Christ...I love you with an intense love that grows with each new day. My heart is yours! To **my gentle and loving daughter Mindy Kent,** forever in my heart, you are one of the nicest and sweetest people I know, you touch peoples' lives with your kind and tender spirit and you are an example of a godly woman...I adore you and I am blest to be your father. I love you. To **my son-in-law Chris Kent,** whom I prefer to call son, which expresses my true feelings; I cannot wait to see how God will use you. He has gifted you for a mighty work. I love you. To my constant companion, ministry partner and the pride of my heart, **my son Ben**...your walk of faith in difficult times has been an inspiration to many including your father, God has a mighty call on your life and you surely are up to it...I love you. To **my sister and brother-in-law Dawn and Steve Sharp,** for your love and support; and to you, Dawn, for your work on the initial manuscript and for believing in her little brother...I love you. To my Dad, **George Stephens** who is part of that cloud of witnesses awaiting the coming Kingdom, and my mom, **Leafie Stephens** and who both worked tirelessly to provide me with opportunities—thanks for your love and support...I love you. To my "big sister," my Aunt **Marilyn Mengel** ("Auntie Mag") for your support and love...I love you.

To our friends and prayer partners for nearly 20 years, **Dan and Joanne Wafer,** your love, prayers and support have seen us through some challenging times.

To **Dean Bratton,** my long time friend and ministry associate, thanks for sharing the vision with me all these years...the day is coming! Also to my friends **Richard Roberts** and **Howard Dayton,** I cannot tell you how your friendship and support for this work has been an encouragement to me, I love you guys!

To my Pastor, **John Carter,** thanks for your input, guidance and support during the difficult personal challenges we faced while this book was a work in progress. Thanks for the good spiritual food you have fed me and my family. You truly walk worthy of your calling. We love you.

To **Don Nori and Don Milam and the people at Destiny Image Publishers,** thank you for your commitment to the Body of Christ to provide them with books to increase their knowledge of the Word. Thank you for keeping Christian publishing a ministry and not just another business. Thank you for keeping the main thing the main thing! May the blessing of the Lord be upon your work! You guys are a class act!

Most of all I wish to thank my **precious Lord and Savior, Jesus Christ.** Thank You for loving me enough to die for me and for being there with me in the difficult and the good times. You picked me up when I failed, dusted me off, set my feet in Your way and put a fire in my Spirit for Your Kingdom that will not be quenched until You establish it here on earth. My life is Yours, use me. I will love and worship You for eternity!!

WHAT OTHER MINISTRY LEADERS ARE SAYING ABOUT THIS BOOK...

Some Christians tend to recoil when they hear the word *prosperity*. In *The Coming Financial Revolution,* Buck clearly delineates the purpose of prosperity—to fund the Kingdom of God.

I really do believe we are on the cusp of a financial revolution. Buck does a tremendous job of skillfully outlining the root of the problem, opening God's Word to define the solution, and encouraging God's people to be obedient.

Howard Dayton, CEO and Co-Founder
Crown Financial Ministries
Gainesville, Georgia

Not only does this book give excellent, step-by-step instructions to help us become good stewards of God's money, but it's written in down-to-earth language that all of us can relate to. Even someone who is swimming in debt can find practical, helpful tips to help them climb out of debt *and stay out.*

With his years of experience as a financial advisor, Buck Stephens knows firsthand that many Christians who are big givers are still not experiencing true financial freedom. What are they missing? And, more importantly, what can they do to change the situation?

Dr. Richard Roberts, President
Oral Roberts University
Tulsa, Oklahoma

There is a Scripture in the Bible that most Christians are unaware of—Ecclesiastes 10:19, which says, "...money answereth all things." Whether we like it or not, money is a necessary part of our lives. In his new book, *The Coming Financial Revolution,* Buck Stephens skillfully deals with this important subject, yet in a practical way that is easy to understand and easy to apply to our everyday lives. The information in this book is vital—not only for you, but for your children and your children's children.

This book will teach you how to have more money, but more importantly, how to do the right thing with it.

Marcus D. Lamb, President/CEO
Daystar Television Network
Dallas, Texas

I believe this work is a masterpiece and a must for all who want to have a clear understanding of how and what to do to effectively prepare for the financial challenges of the future. This book will become a classic!

In every revolution in history, the last area to be conquered was the area of financial resources. Without financial resources, visions become dreams and dreams nightmares. In this book, Buck Stephens tackles the most critical and last remaining area to be dominated by the church—finances, and gives us practical tools to make it a reality.

Dr. Myles Munroe
Best-selling Author and President
BFM International
Nassau, Bahamas

One of satan's most significant strongholds in the body of Christ today is in the area of personal financial management. This book is packed with life-changing knowledge that has the power to move people from bondage to economic victory. With a compelling balance of both wisdom and humor Buck Stephens calls the body of Christ to fulfill her role as stewards of God's resources. The chapter dealing with Jesus' teaching of the ten Minas at Zaccheus' dinner table is one of the most life changing insights I've ever considered.

Rev. John R. Carter, Senior Pastor
Abundant Life Christian Center
East Syracuse, New York
Host of Abundant Living Radio

Good, sound, basic stuff! I think *The Coming Financial Revolution* is an excellent contribution to the field of money management from a Christian perspective, and I certainly would highly recommend it to Christians who need to get these areas of their lives in order.

Rev. Peter Marshall
Evangelist, Author and Founder
Peter Marshall Ministries

CONTENTS

Forewords 15

Preface 19

Introduction 21

Part 1   **Call for the Revolution** 25

Chapter 1   Life Is Like a Sticker Bush! 27

Chapter 2   The World's Best Financial Manual 33

Chapter 3   Brother Hanky for President! 45

Chapter 4   Paralyzed by the Light 59

Chapter 5   The Financial State of the Church 65

Part 2   **Challenges Facing the Revolutionist** 69

Chapter 6   Budgeting—The Famous "B" Word 71

Chapter 7   Debt—The Church's Enemy 75

Chapter 8   Credit and Credit Problems 79

Chapter 9   Money Management 89

Chapter 10   Honesty 93

Chapter 11   Tithing and Giving 97

Chapter 12   Teaching Children 105

Chapter 13   Investing 117

Chapter 14   Financial Planning 133

Chapter 15   Estate Planning 155

Chapter 16   Church Debt 163

Part 3   **Call to Arms** 169

Chapter 17   The Ultimate Identity Theft 171

Chapter 18   Strategy of Satan and God's Plan 193

Chapter 19   Timothy! Guard What Has Been Entrusted To You . . 205

Chapter 20   The Vision of the Financially Faithful Church 217

Chapter 21   Hole-y Purses! 225

Chapter 22   Two Verses 231

Appendix   Induction Papers 235

    The Miracle of Seed Faith 239

FOREWORDS

It is easy to become discouraged if we focus on the statistics in America relating to growing debt and bankruptcies, and shrinking savings and giving. The most disheartening part is that Christians are not exempt from these problems; particularly when you look at the younger generation, the future appears very bleak.

Churches and ministries continue to struggle financially, and, as Buck Stephens says so powerfully, it would be great if ministry leaders would be able to focus more on ministry issues than funding issues. I echo Buck's desire to see money beginning to flow through the church and into God's Kingdom.

The mission of Crown Financial Ministries is to equip people worldwide to learn, apply, and teach God's financial principles so they may know Christ more intimately, be free to serve Him, and help fund *The Great Commission.* We have seen the hearts of God's people change, one by one, and churches transformed, one by one, as they begin to learn what God's Word says about handling, not only 10 percent of their money, but 100 percent of their possessions. We've seen person after person experience God's peace and release from the bondage of materialism.

Some Christians tend to recoil when they hear the word *prosperity*. In *The Coming Financial Revolution,* Buck clearly delineates the purpose of prosperity—to fund the Kingdom of God.

I really do believe we are on the cusp of a financial revolution. Buck does a tremendous job of skillfully outlining the root of the problem, opening God's Word to define the solution, and encouraging God's people to be obedient. I've known Buck as a close friend for many years. I'm confident he's the man to be a leader in this army of revolutionaries. He's an encourager, exhorter, and knows our Lord in a very deep way.

Just as the brave warriors came alongside David to take back the kingdom for the people of God centuries ago, I encourage you to join in the army of fighting men and women to come alongside Buck in this revolution to help fulfill *The Great Commission*.

Howard Dayton, Co-Founder and CEO
Crown Financial Ministries
Gainesville, Georgia

What is the "Financial Revolution" that Buck Stephens is calling Christians to get involved in? First of all, let me say that most of us have been taught that a revolution is *not* a good thing. Aren't revolutions something that only rebels and hotheads get involved in? Christians are supposed to be meek and mild, aren't they?

But, if you really think about it, Christianity itself is a revolutionary movement. Jesus is a revolutionary Leader. And anybody who says he or she is a Christian has already joined the greatest revolution of all time!

So what does Buck Stephens want us to do now? He wants us to have a godly revolution in our finances. He wants us to stop doing things the world's way, by piling up the debts so we can have more "stuff," and start handling our finances the way God teaches us in His Word. Then we can begin to accumulate wealth, not so we can have more "stuff," but so we can support God's work all over the earth.

One statement the author makes has really caught my eye. He says, in essence, if Christians get involve in this "Financial Revolution" and become truly financially free, "ministry leaders will be able to focus on ministry issues and not funding issues."

Can you imagine how that statement strikes my heart? As a ministry leader, I constantly find myself having to deal with funding issues, which sometimes keeps me distracted from dealing with the ministry issues God has called me to deal with. Wouldn't it be wonderful if that situation was reversed?

The problems that Buck Stephens deals with in this book are especially dear to my heart because it was only about a year ago when God spoke to me and said, "My people are suffering under a heavy load of debt." Then the Lord dealt with me to launch an all-out assault on debt.

I went on my television program and began to talk to people about sowing their seeds of faith to God and believing for Him to multiply them back in the form of reducing their debt. The response was overwhelming. And, over the past year, we've received hundreds of testimonies from people who have experienced fantastic debt-reduction miracles through their seed planting.

The Coming Financial Revolution makes it clear that sowing our seeds to God is a fundamental part of godly finances. But there's more to biblical finances than sowing seeds to God.

With his years of experience as a financial advisor, Buck Stephens knows firsthand that many Christians who are big givers are still not experiencing true financial freedom. What are they missing? And, more importantly, what can they do to change the situation?

He says that, first of all, it's important for Christians to develop a financial plan and have proper estate planning. God wants us to be wise in handling our money and to invest it wisely. He wants us to be good stewards over the resources He's given us.

Of course, there's no way we can separate our financial life from the rest of our lives as Christians. Our obedience to the Lord is what brings us His blessings in any area of our lives. And it's hard for Him to bless us financially if we're not walking in obedience to Him in some other area.

Not only does this book give excellent, step-by-step instructions to help us become good stewards of God's money, but it's written in down-to-earth language that all of us can relate to. Even someone who is swimming in debt can find practical, helpful tips to help them climb out of debt *and stay out.*

The Lord has set before us the promised land of financial freedom. He wants us to be free, not only so we can have our needs met and live the abundant life He wants us to live, but so we can reach the world with the gospel. But we can't do that if our hands are tied behind our backs. We can't do that if we don't have the money to do it.

I would encourage anyone who wants to see souls saved, who wants to be able to support the work of the gospel, to join this Financial Revolution today.

Hosea 4:6a says, "My people are destroyed from lack of knowledge." God has given us His personal Financial Manual, the Bible. Let's find out what the Bible says about finances and live our lives that way!

Richard Roberts, President
Oral Roberts University
Tulsa, Oklahoma

PREFACE

The American economy in the last 50 years has seen a marked increase in inflation, personal consumer debt, corporate debt, and financial dishonesty. Most Americans are deeply in debt, and bankruptcies are increasing. The United States government's financial needs are increasing, and it is obvious that the deficit will not be eliminated anytime in the near future. The "national treasure" seems to have turned into the "national debt."

The people of this nation seek peace and comfort, but bondage to materialism and debt has caused 69 percent of them, according to a *USA Today* poll, to be worried about their financial future. In the Hebrew language, the word from the Bible translated "peace" means "nothing missing, nothing broken," yet Americans search for that which is *missing* in their life through the accumulation of wealth, which ironically leaves many families *broken* by the bondage to debt and materialism. We as a nation have become "broke" (as we say) in many ways.

Unfortunately, this is occurring even within the family of God, the Church of the Lord Jesus Christ; among those whom ought to know better, but don't. We as a nation and as a church have broken out of stride with what God originally promised and intended for His people. He promised that we would be "the lender and not the borrower, the head and not the tail"; but we have borrowed, and debt and materialism are wagging us! The way we have been taught and think about money has caused us to err in many ways.

The "people of the Book" in their knowledge of the Book know the least about the second most talked about subject in the Bible—money and possessions. God gives us His wisdom regarding the use of money and possessions to accomplish His purpose. Successful strategies of Wall

Street today were recorded in the Word of God thousands of years ago; the pitfalls of today are there as well.

Yet as we continue our quest for prosperity, we have forgotten about obedience. But can we claim one without the other? After studying the Word on the subject of money and possessions, this author has concluded that obedience and prosperity not only correlate but actually mean the same thing! You can't have true prosperity without obedience in all areas of life. Subsequently, you cannot have peace without this kind of prosperity, a prosperity where nothing is missing and nothing is broken!

We now live in a time when the influence of the people of God is growing in America, when ministers of the gospel are being hailed by secular media as some of the most influential people in this world. It is a time where best-selling books on the secular charts are those that teach God's principles to a society that has long shunned God and even thrown Him out of their schools and governmental buildings.

Within these people are a growing number of revolutionists whom Jesus spoke of when He called them the "forceful" (NIV) or "violent" (KJV) who will take the Kingdom by force! (see Matt. 11:12).

This Kingdom about which He said that "from the days of John the Baptist has been forcefully advancing" is nearing, when the King of that Kingdom, the Lord Jesus Christ will return to establish His Kingdom here on earth as He promised. The Eternal King is sending His forces out to do His will to prepare for and bring about that eternal Kingdom.

One of the last great bastions of the enemy involves the financial, yet the coming King has declared that "the silver is Mine and the gold is Mine" and that He will "shake all nations" (see Hag. 2:7-8) and return what is rightfully His into the control of His people.

These revolutionists through faith, education, obedience, and accountability will fulfill the prophetic word, "The wealth of the sinner is laid up for the just" (Prov. 13:22 KJV), and use that wealth to establish the throne of Christ and bring about the Kingdom of Heaven on earth.

The cry of "call to arms" rings out among the people of God.

Who will join them?

INTRODUCTION

I thank you for your time to read and consider the content of this book; and I do not believe it is any accident that you are about to read this book. I have fervently prayed that God would put it into the hands of only those whom He has called to be part of this coming revolution. Let me give you a little background so that as you read this book, you will be able to better understand the purpose for which it was written. If you are not certain you wish to read this book, I encourage you to first read the Preface and the last chapter (22), which is a bit of a summary of what is contained herein. Then when you read the entire book, read that chapter again.

There have been a number of excellent how-to or financial advice books written. The purpose in writing this book was not to reinvent the wheel. This book is more of a "Why?" book, calling God's people to become financially faithful according to the Scriptures and then pointing them to resources that have been effective tools in helping the Body achieve this goal. I have learned that people need tools, not just advice, to learn.

In the years of making presentations in various places in the Christian community, I have been frequently asked if there is any way that people could get their hands on the information that I presented. It has been suggested so often that I incorporate the information into book form, that I decided to do just that, or to, like Jonah, risk being swallowed by a whale. I never set out to be, or imagined myself as an author, but then again, I never expected to be led where God has led me. Let me state at the outset that this is not "my" book but "His" because it comes straight from His Word. I am simply the tool He has used to get it to His people. The ease and manner in which these words became a published book was so obviously orchestrated that those of us who have been involved with its publication recognize it as truly a God thing! It is in your hands now, I know, because He desires it to be.

In recent years, I saw the effectiveness of my ministry increase as I began to partner with the Crown Financial Ministries small group study developed by my friend Howard Dayton. I would, in preparation for ministry at a church or organization, first equip them with this program to begin a financial ministry in that body after a call was made to the stewards there. I would then speak to that body of believers and make the call to financial faithfulness, directing God's people to the source of their training, which was now an established ready-to-go program at their church or organization. This program has become known as "The Advancing the Kingdom Weekend." The results have been so miraculous and often surprising to even me, the messenger, that I know the anointing of the Lord is upon it.

My qualifications are not rooted in the fact that I have been a financial advisor and counselor in the Christian community for many years; frankly, I am just another "broken vessel" whom the Lord is using, or as I like to say, "just one of the Lord's 'cracked pots.'" The Word of God says that God uses the foolish to confound the wise. It may be referring to me. I am special only because Jesus makes me so. I wear His robe of righteousness that has covered my unrighteousness. Do not look to me at all, only to Him; for I am just a tool in the hand of the Master. I too have qualified as a "Brother Hanky" who you will meet in Chapter 3. It is my hope that with Christ's help I too can become a "president" in His Kingdom like my readers will be called to do.

God is daily expanding His ministry through His servant son. I have become more of a "finangelist" (financial evangelist) than an advisor. When the call is made to a body of believers in tandem with an ongoing financial training program, the results are phenomenal. I have found that without the call to the Body, the Church can experience a very sluggish response, for most people do not know the things that are taught in God's Word, which are included in this book. The Church has conformed itself individually and corporately to the world's systems in many ways because of their lack of knowledge of the Word's systems and principles. And unfortunately, the Church, for the most part, does not know that they don't know!

I am always telling church leaders, "They don't know that they don't know!" They need to be educated regarding God's financial principles. We need to be "transformed by the renewing of our minds" or in most cases, the education of our minds, in this area. "Don't copy the behavior and customs of this world, but let God transform you into a new person by *changing the way you think*. Then you will know what God wants you to *do*, and you will know how good and pleasing and perfect His will really is" (Rom. 12:2 NLT, emphasis added).

I view this book as a "call to arms," to call the Body out of "Hankianism" (a term I made up—see definition in Chapter 3) and into the abundant life Christ has promised us as faithful and obedient stewards. The book is also a resource to churches, organizations, and believers directing them to the tools they need to begin financial ministries in their churches.

It is my goal to get this message into the hands of every church leader and steward of God in the United States and Canada, for I believe that it comes directly from the Holy Spirit, "for such a time as this" (Esther 4:14b).

Won't you be part of this great move of God among His people? Won't you help spread this message? Encourage others to read this book and sign on to this mighty revolution.

This book is designed to be an "easy read" without a lot of dry financial strategies, statistics, and advice. I hope you enjoy it, but most of all I hope it will challenge you as the information contained herein challenged me. These principles will change your life as they have and are continuing to change Andrea's and mine. We are a work in progress; God is not done with us and is opening new revelations as we continue this "faith walk" of our lives. It is my hope that you too will become part of a revolution now beginning in the Church in the area of finances and funding the great commission of Christ.

In the service of the King,
Buck Stephens, servant son

PART 1

CALL FOR THE REVOLUTION

CHAPTER 1

LIFE IS LIKE A STICKER BUSH!

Why am I doing this? I can't believe that I am actually sitting down and writing a book about all this financial stuff and that a top-notch, well-known publisher actually wants to publish it! Lord, is this what You really want me to do—to share all the things You have shown me? No one wants to hear about finances—a really boring topic to most people. They think financial advisors are dull! (Well, I'm not the sharpest tool in Your shed, but I'm definitely not dull!) Oh, and I, myself, have made a lot of mistakes in this area over the years. Why are You choosing me? Some might think I, of all people, should not be writing this. I agree with them. Surely, Lord, someone else would be better!

Oh...excuse me...I was just having a talk with my Lord. Well, I guess I am into this now. There is no one else here to do this but me, and uh...you're here reading...it's just you and me, so I guess I will try to do my best. Okay.

Lord, this is Your book. You lead and I'll write. These nice folks, Your people—Lord, they are looking on, and they want to see what I am writing. So fill me with Your Spirit; leave out anything of me. Here we go!

Hi! I am Buck Stephens, alias Jeremiah or Jonah or maybe even Moses. (Moses and I both had an encounter with a bush...you'll see!) Yes sir, I could have been the lead singer in a group called "The No Can Do's." I envision myself more like Gideon though. Like Gideon, when the Lord called me, I said, "Yeah...right! Me, Lord? You can't be talking to me!" Then, like Gideon, I made Him prove it; and just for good measure, to prove it again! (see Judg. 6:36-40). Much to my surprise, He did! So then I was stuck. That's why I am here.

I used to believe in fairy tales!

I believed my checkbook would balance all by itself, and that I would never run out of money at the end of the month. I believed that people would always be honest and fair in their dealings with me, and when I got into trouble there would be my fairy godmother to bail me out, especially if I spoke the right formula. (Actually, I thought God would. I don't really have a fairy godmother.) He always made me work though. No magic wands, that's for sure! The only wand He waved, He used on my backside! ("For whom the Lord loves He chastens" [Heb. 12:6a NKJV].) I guess He loves me a lot!

What do you expect from a guy who as a kid thought that if he could run fast enough through the sticker bush, he wouldn't get pricked? I set out to prove it, tried it with my friends looking on and…yeeow! Just to be sure, I tried it again, brilliant boy! Strike two! I did stop after two, but just so you know, I still think I just didn't run fast enough.

Mom said, "What happened to your legs?" I didn't tell her…I knew she wouldn't understand. Dad just looked and smiled. He never said anything. I somehow think he knew. Maybe he had tried it! Maybe the ability to run at an unscathable (or unscratchable) speed is male theory.

Well, little boys grow up, and they enter the real world. It's a world full of surprises—salespersons and creditors looking for prey, medical bills, and broken-down cars. There I am in the midst of them all, flying by the seat of my pants. Yes siree, Bob! Winging it like a pro! My bag is packed with Algebra, Geometry, and that modern math stuff, but I don't have a clue about how to balance my checkbook or how interest can bury me. I've got this gorgeous blue-eyed bride. We don't need money; all we need is love, right? That's what the Beatles said. Well, it's kinda right— until we need some money, then we're gonna find out whose fault it is that the well is dry—hers or mine. Where did it go? I haven't a clue! All those nice people who wanted to loan me money suddenly had a personality change and started sending me nasty letters and calling me on the phone at all hours. Then the arguments began!

The point is, we may have graduated from high school and some of us have college degrees; but nowhere along the way did anyone ever teach us how to handle our own personal money, to develop a budget, or to even balance a checkbook. Of course, you could always try using the two checkbook system. When one is goofed up, you just switch to the other one until that one gets goofed up, and then you switch back to the original one again. By now, you probably have cleared all checks in that one so you can start over with the balance on the bank statement. Am I talking to anyone here? I know you're out there!

Life *is* like a sticker bush!

Some of us think that if we work harder, take on another job, run faster in life, do it our way, then somehow things will be different and we won't get pricked this time! But then we might say as the writer did in Ecclesiastes 2:11, "Then I looked on all the works my hands had done and on the labor in which I had toiled; and indeed all was vanity and grasping for the wind. There was no profit under the sun" (NKJV). Do you ever feel like a "not for profit" organization? I have!

Maybe if we ignore the problem, it will go away. Einstein once said that the definition of *insanity* is doing the same thing over and over yet expecting a different result. Yet many of us continue to do the same thing over and over because we just don't know any better. Maybe we have never learned because we have never been taught or have never taken the time to learn.

Excuse me, readers, I just heard one of you say that he is glad that Christians who need help handling their money have resources like this book available. (Of course, he personally does not need any help.) He has no debt and has accumulated substantial wealth besides. Let me just say to that reader that this book is for him too, and we will be getting to him in just a little bit. ("Great!" his wife just said. "Read on, Honey!")

The truth is, there is little difference between the way God's stewards handle money and the way the world does. *The reason is that we have been taught by the world how to handle money and not by the Word.* For example, I remember when I first started my career in the financial field—I was trained by financial companies regarding how to borrow and to leverage myself as high as I could get. They taught me investment strategies that, as I grew wiser over the years and asked those questions they did not like me asking, I saw benefited primarily them.

Once, when I conducted a financial faithfulness weekend at a church in a metropolitan area, the pastor shared with me that one of his elders, a senior man who had known the Lord for many years, came to him asking, "Pastor, should we really be talking about money in the church, especially in Sunday morning services?" Is talking about money in the church really a taboo topic? Many people think it is.

The *Dallas Morning News* on page 1G, Feb. 12, 2000, reported in an article "Keeping Up Face" that according to a survey conducted by a major denomination, "Money is a taboo topic at church. Almost half of Christians (48%) believe it is inappropriate to discuss money and material possessions at church. However, money and material possessions are among the most frequently discussed topics in the Bible. How many Christians know that? Two percent according to the survey." This explains why the financial issue is the silent crisis in the church. It is the enemy's secret weapon, binding God's people and ministries and preventing them from reaching their full potential in spreading the gospel of Jesus Christ. Financial shortage is the source of ministry paralysis. Eighty-five percent of all pastors polled by Crown Financial Ministries in a survey felt unequipped to handle this issue in the church. Many are suffering from financial stress themselves and are afraid to confront it in their own lives. Howard Dayton, co-founder with Larry Burkett and now CEO of Crown Financial Ministries, noted a striking statistic in his book, *Your Money Counts* (copyright 1996, Publisher Crown Ministries). There are more than 2,350 verses in the Bible about handling money and possessions, which does not even include verses on seedtime and harvest. When you contrast that with a subject like prayer, in which there are about 500 verses in the Bible, you begin to realize the significance that finances are to God. Yet, according to the Crown Financial Ministries' survey, 90 percent of churches have no program to equip the steward to meet the obligation given to him by the Master in Luke chapter 19.

Significant? Yes!

Christians need to be trained in this area with more than just the occasional one-shot, hit-and-run seminar, special class, or sermon series—been there, done that! Then afterward, things go back to the way they were before. We have to get serious about financial issues, and church leaders must catch hold of the vision and take the necessary steps to align themselves and their ministries with it. We as ministry leaders must stop pleading for money, and instead teach our people how to accumulate it! We need to plant seeds of financial faithfulness in the stewards, and as they come in line with biblical principles and prosper, the ministry work will share in the harvest.

I did the one-shot seminar thing for awhile. People said the meetings were great and just what they needed, but I almost quit because they were ineffective in bringing about significant lasting change to bodies of believers. I never saw the success I am seeing now when I call the church or organization to financial faithfulness after I have equipped them with the necessary tools to bring about change through an ongoing program of teaching biblical principles of financial stewardship.

That is what the Lord has asked me to convey in this book—to call and to help equip the Church in preparation for the coming Kingdom!

We have a choice!

We can continue to keep running through that sticker bush, hoping that eventually things will work out the way we want it to; or we can stop, and like Moses did, listen to what God wants to say to us through that bush.

CHAPTER 2

THE WORLD'S BEST FINANCIAL MANUAL

S till with me? That's great! Now I hear some of you more skeptical ones out there checking off, "One, two, three, four…" Yeah, I hear you counting! Whether you take my word for it, or keep on counting for yourselves, there really are over 2,350 verses in the Bible about money and possessions. Hey, but continue counting—anything that gets you into the Word of God! If we all spent more time in the Word, researching what it has to say on different topics, this issue of money would not come as such a surprise to us. The devil keeps us so busy with other pursuits that he prevents us from reading what God has to say to us. In fact, I believe we are talking about the biggest problem facing the Church today. Yes, I said, "the biggest." Moreover, it is also the most neglected. Why do I think so? I think so because no other issue affects more aspects of the life of Christians and of the ministry of the Church!

Listen to me. I am about to tell you a secret! It is an intelligence report from Holy Spirit headquarters! The secret is that the disrupted and unorganized finances of the Body of Christ is what the enemy uses to render us ineffective in ministry, to disable us from living the abundant life that Jesus promised, and to rip at the very core of our marriages and families! The silent weapon of the enemy is bondage to debt, the pursuit of wealth, and the fear of losing that wealth. Why? It breaks our focus on God—that's why! It preoccupies us. It is the silent yet deadly subject of the Church.

We hear sermons about giving, tithing, and not robbing God—all focusing on 10 percent of the believer's income. As a financial advisor for nearly 30 years working with Christians, I tell you this is not where the problem is. The problem is in how the other 90 percent of income is handled. *How the 10 percent is handled is a symptom of how the 90 percent is handled!* We don't hear sermons on the 90 percent because 85 percent of pastors polled in that survey we talked about, feel unequipped to preach and teach on this subject. In fact, many pastors and ministry leaders are in the same boat, and boy, is it a'rockin! I have had pastors admit to me that they resisted my ministry because they were not willing to look at their own personal finances or those of the church they pastored.

Some ministries have mismanaged money, where in the pursuit of "excellence" within the ministry, they crossed over into "extravagance." (We will talk more about this subject later.) One time, an associate came to me seeking my counsel in how to counsel another individual. Over $50,000 of credit card debt had buried this man and his family. In reviewing this tough situation, I asked my associate if this individual had talked with his pastor, to which he replied, "Buck, he *is* the pastor!" In fact, to make matters worse, he had used the credit to supplement his support in a church that was not supporting him. Ouch! Am I talking to anyone out there?

Over the years, three predominant theories of handling money have developed within the church. God has seen fit in my training, for this time in my life, to expose me to all three theories in practice. These three—poverty theology, prosperity theology, and stewardship theology appear on the following spectrum:

/ ——————————— / ——————————— /

Poverty	Stewardship	Prosperity
Theology	Theology	Theology

Poverty theology was prevalent during the 1800s and early 1900s, but I do occasionally run into those who still believe this way. In regard to money, the poverty theologist believes that it is godly to be poor because the Christian should be disgusted with worldly gain. At the same time, the Christian is encouraged to be benevolent. My question is: If you are poor, how can you also be benevolent when you are the one needing the benevolence? Although, there is some Scripture to support this view, it is not entirely biblical. How can you be a blessing to others if you personally are not blessed?

Listen! If you want to help the poor, the best way to start is by not being one of them!

Prosperity theology, on the other hand, simply states, "You *have* not because you *ask* not!" Hey, now that is biblical, isn't it? Jesus said it Himself! The problem is that the *pure* prosperity theologist takes this theory too far, claiming that a transaction binds God to give you what you *want* (notice the emphasis on the word *want*). This person follows Christ only because of what it will bring to him in the form of material prosperity. He uses the Word for his own personal gain. If you follow the formula, then great riches will result. If you are not receiving riches, then you must not believe. Although there may be an element of truth here, it is often carried too far, because it is practiced, as I often say, "without understanding"—leading the steward to disillusion and discouragement. I have counseled countless people who need to, as one of my Bible professors used to say, "Look at the *whole* Scripture on this subject if you want to understand what God says."

Even though these two theories are based in part on Scripture, the true poverty or prosperity theologist is actually hard to find. There are people today who have been "labeled" by others as proponents of one or the other theory, but their actual beliefs are often distorted on websites and books by "self-appointed judges for God" who base their information on secondhand information (hearsay) and the secular media reports (who do not like the "religious right" and seek to discredit anyone having success or who calls them to a higher standard).

When I was growing up, I heard all types of criticism against ministers of the gospel, and unfortunately, it tainted my views of them. However, since I have grown older and wiser, I have learned to never accept anything until I have checked it out for myself, which is how I have learned that hearsay cannot be trusted, even among Christians. I discovered later in life that many of the accusations I heard while growing up were inaccurate because there was a lack of understanding or they were just downright false.

Caution: There have been many who have labeled some believers as "name it and claim it," which in reality is a misunderstanding and exaggeration of what they teach. The Bible teaches, as we will see throughout this book, that if we follow God's plan with our finances, we will prosper and be blessed (see Ps. 35:27, 3 John 2). However, it also teaches that *prosperity requires obedience and requires it even after we have prospered to retain* *that prosperity.* Psalm 35:27b says that the Lord "has pleasure in the prosperity of His servant" (NKJV). Remember, stewardship theology teaches that *prosperity results from the faithful administration of our money,* which basically means following the Word of God in regard to handling money and possessions. Deuteronomy 29:9 says, "Carefully follow the terms of this covenant, so that you may prosper in everything you do." *Prosperity or wealth is the result of our obedience!* Ministers who teach this concept have often been wrongly dubbed as prosperity theologists. I recently read a Christian book that did just this. The author criticized one of God's anointed preachers who has stood the Bible test and the test of time and whose ministry has been blessed in ways most of us only dream of experiencing. He was criticized in a very backhanded, unloving way. According to Scripture, this is a dangerous thing to do in and of itself. King David himself was afraid to touch "God's anointed," even though many people thought Saul deserved to be "touched." Irregardless, David would not do it! He knew the judgment of God would rest upon him for doing so (see 1 Sam. 26:9; Ps. 105:15). It is God's responsibility and authority to rise up or anoint and to take down, not ours.

Reader, do you ever criticize your pastor? "Touch not God's anointed!" Your pastor has a tougher Judge than you, so you should pray for him to walk according to the Spirit. If he doesn't live accordingly, you need to find another shepherd.

I recognized that the information that the author used to criticize this minister had been based on half-truths, had been obtained from secular media reports, and was received secondhand. Remember, the media's agenda, for the most part, is to discredit us, providing them an excuse for not listening. The fact is, my brother was wrong in his information and wrong in his criticism—in fact, so wrong that it was actually slander. Furthermore, I know that he is not even personally acquainted with this minister or his ministry, which God has blessed for many years and is still blessing. In addition, this ministry has poured millions of dollars back into the Kingdom and has seen a harvest of an untold number of souls as a result.

But, in just a couple of sentences, slander that questioned another ministry's motives and ethics has been forever recorded in this author's book leaving a black mark in the readers' minds against someone whom the Lord loves dearly and with whom the author will someday live in eternity. Even if the author sees the error of his ways, he will not be able to erase those words. Labels pigeonhole people and are usually inaccurate. Often, those people who are critical of another minister or ministry do not have a ministry whose effect is as far reaching as the ministry they are criticizing. I believe from my years of experience working with different ministries that this critical spirit is rooted in the sin of covetousness.

Some of you may be saying, "We are supposed to 'test' the spirits and to expose false teaching," and with that I wholeheartedly agree (see 1 John 4:1-3). However, we must test the spirit the way Jesus did in Matthew chapter 7. Jesus first tells us not to judge, saying that we will be judged in the same manner in which we have judged others. (That's scary all by itself.) He, in this passage, also cautions us from developing the condition I call "plank-eye" (seeing the speck in your brother's eye when you have a beam in your own), and He goes on to talk about the false teacher issue saying:

> *Beware of false prophets, which come to you in sheep's clothing, but inwardly they are ravening wolves.* **Ye shall know them by their fruits.** *Do men gather grapes of thorns, or figs of thistles? Even so every good tree bringeth forth good fruit; but a corrupt tree bringeth forth evil fruit.* **A good tree cannot bring forth evil fruit; neither can a corrupt tree bring forth good fruit.** *Every tree that bringeth not forth good fruit is hewn down, and cast into the fire.* **Wherefore by their fruits ye shall know them** (Matthew 7:15-20 KJV, emphasis added).

What were the fruits of Jesus' ministry? The test for any ministry is to determine if it has the same fruit as the ministry of the Lord Jesus whom they serve. The fruits of Jesus' ministry are recorded three times in Matthew and Luke:

> *And Jesus went about all Galilee,* **teaching** *in their synagogues, and* **preaching the gospel** *of the kingdom, and* **healing** *all manner of sickness and all manner of disease among the people* (Matthew 4:23 KJV, emphasis added).

> *And Jesus went about all the cities and villages,* **teaching** *in their synagogues, and* **preaching the gospel** *of the kingdom, and* **healing**

every sickness and every disease among the people (Matthew 9:35 KJV, emphasis added).

*And they departed, and went through the towns, **preaching the gospel,** and healing every where* (Luke 9:6 KJV, emphasis added).

There is the test! Is there teaching? Preaching the gospel of the Kingdom? Healing? Are lives being changed and affected for Christ? Has the ministry stood the test of time, or has it been cut down by God? (Remember, He is the only one who should have a saw.) Perhaps you do not agree with all a minister teaches, and maybe the minister isn't perfect (he's not; he needed a Savior too). God, as I said in the Introduction, uses imperfect vessels; therefore, we can always find fault with any ministry, including mine. Ministers make mistakes too, just like you do. However, God can still use anyone, even as He still uses the brother who wrote these unity-breaking words of error. (Notice I am not mentioning his name! I would not touch God's anointed.)

Just another thought here before we move on.

Paul in Ephesians chapter 4 writes, urging the Ephesians to "live a life worthy of the calling you have received" (vs. 1). One of the evidences he gives of "walking worthy of our calling" listed in verses 2 and 3 is "keeping the unity of the Spirit through the bond of peace." Criticism and a judgmental attitude will break the unity of the Body and it has done so, which must grieve the Holy Spirit greatly. The subject of money and prosperity has been and continues to be a major area that the enemy targets to break our unity in Christ! I could write a whole book on this subject itself. *We should never tear down another ministry while praying that God bless our own.* Whatsoever you sow, you shall reap, and the same manner in which you judge, you shall be judged. Remember also to "touch not God's anointed"!

How about you? Are you walking worthy of your calling? All of us, it seems, have fallen down in this area at one time or another. I know I have!

Hmm…talk amongst yourselves!

Now back to the subject at hand.

It is rare indeed to find such a Christian who is a pure poverty or prosperity theologian, but I must confess, I have talked to some! They are out there! Few believers would actually recognize their names because God does not bless their ministries (unless you consider getting poorer a blessing to the poverty theologist). They may succeed for a time, but then they come crashing down. The poverty theologist runs out of money and closes his doors, and the prosperity theologist's material world comes crashing down on him for God's hand is not on him either. Standing the test of time and the Word is a good indication of God's anointing. So *"touch not God's anointed"*!

Understand that the true prosperity teacher seeks personal prosperity as the main goal, not prosperity for the advancement of the Kingdom of Jesus Christ. I remember two prosperity teachers in the 1980s who gained a lot of followers. But then, God got out the saw. Today, they are nowhere to be found. Remember, "Riches and honor come from You, oh Lord, and You are the ruler of all mankind: Your hand controls power and might and it is at Your discretion that men are made great and given strength" (1 Chron. 29:12 LB). It is God who is responsible for judging a ministry or a minister. Jesus said that "by their fruits ye shall know them" (Matt. 7:20 KJV). If you have questions about a ministry, and God is blessing them, then let God handle it!

Most Christians will find themselves on the line somewhere in between the poverty and prosperity theologies. So, what's the truth?

If we look at the whole Scripture, we find that stewardship theology combines the elements of truth from the other two theologies. Simply stated, stewardship theology says that *possessions are privileges, that they are not our own, and that prosperity is the result of faithfully administering our talents (see Matt. 25), our minas (see Luke 19), or in today's terms, our money!*

Our faithfulness to what? Faithfulness to God and to the process He has given us in the Word for handling our money and accumulating wealth for His purposes. This takes discipline! This takes knowledge! Many are declaring God's provision in faith and yet not realizing it is coming because they are not disciplined or trained in handling God's provision. I hear many Christians today saying, "Money cometh!" And that is a truth taught in God's Word. He promises to provide, but there is more to it than "Money cometh"! What do I mean?

Daffy Buck says, "Money cometh, but it go-eth because we don't know-eth!"

We need to understand what God's Word teaches about handling money and possessions; to not only receive, but also to retain and manage the blessings God sends to us.

One of the main messages of the Bible relative to money is taught by the great teacher Himself. Jesus tells us in Matthew 6:24 that "you cannot serve both God and money." For many years, I believed that this verse was for the wealthy. It is, after all, found in the passage where Jesus talks about laying up treasures in Heaven instead of here on earth. It was not until later in life, however, that I realized that this verse is speaking to all of us. If you are faced with an electric bill, the need for groceries, a better car, or paying the rent to Old Snidely Whiplash, where do you think your focus is if you do not have the money? Is it on improving your relationship with the Lord, or on sharing Christ with that friend, neighbor, or coworker?

I don't think so!

Why do you think programs at your church are canceled? It is usually because there is either a lack of money, or a lack of people, or both. If people are in bondage to debt or to the pursuit of a living, they not only cannot give, but neither do they have the time or the focus to be involved in the ministry efforts. Which master are we then serving—God or money?

A second important message of the Bible is: Bondage to debt is bad. I am amazed as to how many Christians and pastors do not know Proverbs 22:7: "The rich rule over the poor, and the borrower is servant to the lender" (NIV). Anyone out there identify with this?

If you have ever owed money, you know what this is talking about. The Bible tells us to "owe no one anything except to love one another" (Rom. 13:8 NKJV). The Church today is in bondage to financial debt, individually and corporately. The focus is often on earning a living and paying off debt rather than on ministering. Christ calls us to evangelism, yet we spend our time on worldly temporal things!

The most important message in the Bible regarding finances simply put is this: *It is not ours!* Psalm 24:1 says, "The earth is the Lord's, and everything in it!"

Now, here is something for those of you who may not have debt and have accumulated some wealth: To whom much is given, much is expected (see Luke 12:48). The fact is, according to Scripture, everything belongs to God! Think of something that does not belong to God. First Chronicles 29:11b states, "Everything in the heaven and Earth is Yours, O Lord, and this is Your Kingdom" (LB). The fact is, whatever we have *is* His. *We are simply the custodians or the stewards of His possessions.* So many of us think that what we have is ours. Listen, that viewpoint is not biblical!

We need to get our minds out of ownership and into stewardship!

I personally understand this concept. Let me illustrate it for you.

I have been a financial advisor for years. I regularly look at clients' statements and help them manage their money. Even though I manage it and make decisions according to the goals and directives of my clients, I never think of it as mine. I am responsible with it, but I am mentally and emotionally detached from its ownership.

Let's consider another life example. Pastor Rick Warren, author of the *New York Times* best-seller, *The Purpose Driven Life,* and pastor of the Saddleback Church in Lake Forest, California experienced what I refer to as a "suddenly blessing" when his book became an incredible success and touched and is still touching the lives of many. Rick is the first to admit that he never expected the book to be the success that it has been. The book was recognized as "the best-selling non-fiction hardback book in history." I believe that its success shows just how hungry the world is for purpose (which we will talk more about in Chapter 17) and spiritual direction. I believe it also shows that the influence of God's people is increasing and will continue to do so all the more as this financial revolution of God's people gets a full head of steam.

Rick has a personal story about this "suddenly blessing" which he has told publicly and has allowed me to share here, not to call attention to his stewardship and generosity, but because I believe it so well illustrates the proper attitude concerning God's ownership of our money and possessions.

The Purpose Driven Life generated sales of about a million books a month and generated substantial royalties paid to Pastor Rick and his wife, Kay. Rick and Kay, because they knew the Word, recognized Who the source of the blessing was and Whose book royalties they really were. They were therefore led to reinvest those into the Kingdom to further advance the gospel. The Holy Spirit led them to bless and again plant seed in the ministry in which they have faithfully served through some difficult financial times since 1980. They decided not to change their lifestyle and continued to drive the same cars (Rick's car at the time of this writing is four years old) and live as they had lived before they received this "suddenly blessing." They then calculated what they had received in pay as pastor since the founding of the church and planted that amount of money back in Saddleback Church by returning all pay they have ever received back to the church. Rick now continues serving as pastor without pay. The same stewardship and generosity they exhibited before their blessing continues as they continue to tithe and give generously to the work of the Kingdom, just as the Word of God teaches us. I believe God used and blessed Rick and Kay because they had shown Him so clearly they were prepared to handle it...His way!

God will not give us a blessing we are not prepared to handle or will not handle according to His directives. How we handle our money through the lean times will show how we will handle the money through the blessing times. How we think of the money during lean times will be how we think about money during the blessing times.

Yes, as I said, we need to get our minds out of ownership and into stewardship and begin to view our money as God's money! Rick and Kay's faithfulness illustrates this.

We need to think of the money that God has given us to manage as His, and to manage it according to His directives in ways that advance His Kingdom. He has not left us clueless either, for He fully intended the

Church to train His servants to handle His money. He wrote the Financial Manual with more than 2,350 financial verses in it!

When Jesus taught through parables, over half of them dealt with money and possessions, and one is especially hard-hitting to the Body of Christ today. Come with me to the next chapter, sit back, strap on your safety belt, and get ready for a lesson taught by Jesus Himself.

Oh, how I love Him!

CHAPTER 3

BROTHER HANKY FOR PRESIDENT!

Plese get out your Financial Manuals and turn to Luke chapter 19, verses 11 through 27. That's right! I said, "Financial Manuals." Besides many other things, your Bible is a financial manual. That's what the cover on the Bible in my office says—"Financial Manual." This manual was written through men and authored by the Financial Advisor who created this world and inspired its financial systems.

Pretty credible, don't you think?

I don't know about you, but I love God's Word. I love reading it, studying it, and letting God reveal things through it. I have a "red-lettered" edition of the Bible, and I especially perk up when the words in my Bible turn red! That means my Lord Jesus Christ spoke the words I am reading! Wow! Red gives those words some level of credibility—the words of the Great Teacher, the Son of the God who created all things, and the Savior of the world! When my Bible's words turn red, I know for certain that I cannot challenge those words in any way. In this particular passage from Luke, except for the introduction in verse 11, all the words are red! All are the spoken words of Christ! Let's read it before we go on further.

While they were listening to this, He went on to tell them a parable, because He was near Jerusalem and the people thought that the kingdom of God was going to appear at once. He said: "A man of noble birth went to a distant country to have himself appointed king and then to return. So he called ten of his servants and gave them ten minas. 'Put this money to work,' he said, 'until I come back.' But his subjects hated him and sent a delegation after him to say, 'We don't want this man to be our king.' He was made king, however, and returned home. Then he sent for the servants to whom he had given the money, in order to find out what they had gained with it. The first one came and said, 'Sir, your mina has earned ten more.' 'Well done, my good servant!' his master replied. 'Because you have been trustworthy in a very small matter, take charge of ten cities.' The second came and said, 'Sir, your mina has earned five more.' His master answered, 'You take charge of five cities.' Then another servant came and said, 'Sir, here is your mina; I have kept it laid away in a piece of cloth. I was afraid of you, because you are a hard man. You take out what you did not put in and reap what you did not sow.' His master replied, 'I will judge you by your own words, you wicked servant! You knew, did you, that I am a hard man, taking out what I did not put in, and reaping what I did not sow? Why then didn't you put my money on deposit, so that when I came back, I could have collected it with interest?' Then he said to those standing by, 'Take his mina away from him and give it to the one who has ten minas.' 'Sir,' they said, 'he already has ten!' He replied, 'I tell you that to everyone who has, more will be given, but as for the one who has nothing, even what he has will be taken away. But those enemies of mine who did not want me to be king over them—bring them here and kill them in front of me'" (Luke 19:11-27).

It is interesting to note that Jesus told this parable immediately after a man exhibited his faith in Him by making a change in the way he handled his money. Zacchaeus, the dishonest tax collector, proclaimed his belief in Jesus and subsequently gave evidence of that profession by becoming faithful in his finances. You know Zacchaeus, the "wee little man who climbed up in a sycamore tree for Jesus he wanted to see," like we sang about in Sunday school. "Jesus said, 'Zacchaeus, you come down, for I'm going to your house today.'" Bring back any Sunday school memories? Well, whether it does or not, Jesus and His disciples went to Zacchaeus' house and had dinner.

Zacchaeus stood up after dinner and declared his faith in Christ; then he gave evidence of that faith through his finances. He promised to change his dishonest ways and to make restitution.

Evidence of faith through finances—that's what we are talking about here!

Let's look at this dinner conversation a bit more closely.

The disciples were excited because they thought that the Kingdom of God was very near. In fact, they believed it was Kingdom eve! Yes, they believed that Jesus would head into Jerusalem, rally the Jews, defeat the Romans, and send them home packing. Jesus would become King, and they would all land themselves a comfortable job in the King's court. What a deal! Even the tax collectors were now listening to Jesus. The disciples thought they were really on a roll! Imagine how you would feel if even the IRS was on your side! Jesus knew what they were thinking and took the opportunity to teach them that the Kingdom was not to be established at this time because there was still work to be done!

While still in Zacchaeus' house, Jesus began to teach them again with a parable—the parable we know as the Parable of the Ten Minas. In this story, Jesus spoke of a man of noble birth who was traveling to a distant land to have himself crowned king. Once appointed king, he would return. Does this ring a bell? Who was soon going away to have Himself crowned King? Yes, Jesus was! He was talking about Himself here in this parable. Do not forget this point as we go on in the text.

Now, because this nobleman (Jesus) was going away for some time, he needed to make arrangements to have his "stuff" taken care of while he was away. He needed someone to oversee his affairs and to manage his estate. He needed to put his wealth in the "trust" of someone. Jesus tells us that this nobleman called ten of his servants and gave them each a mina, which was about three month's wages. Note here that the master gave each of these ten servants, equal amounts. That means that each of them had equal ability to be successful with the money. So while many of us may say, "I'm just not good with money. I just don't have the ability," that thinking is just not biblical! It's right here in this passage! The Master gives each one the same ability and also gives them instructions on how to put it to work. He says, "Invest"! He is very pragmatic here and is actually saying, "Take care of My business." They are to take care of business "until I come back."

The implication here is that the servants were to invest these minas according to the master's instructions, and then to give an account of how they handled them when the master returned. A major part of taking care of the master's business was managing His money! *They were given instructions on what to do, and the master expected them to be successful.* That is why He, as we shall see, will punish the unsuccessful ones. The

Word tells us in Deuteronomy 8:18 that God has given us the power to gain wealth as a confirmation of the covenant He has made with us. We have the ability to be successful, and with the proper instruction and training, we can be successful. The Master expects it!

In verse 14, Jesus warned that He, the Messiah was going to be rejected, just as the nobleman in the illustration was rejected by the people as their king. He warned His disciples that He would be rejected and that they must engage themselves in faithful service to the Master's wealth.

Despite the rejection of the people, the nobleman was anointed king in a distant land. Now in order to be anointed king, there must be someone who has a greater authority that qualifies him to anoint a king—usually the reigning king, or a spiritual authority. It was usually the father king of the newly anointed son king. Such was the case here. Jesus was going away to have Himself anointed King by the only authority who could do so—the God of the universe, His Father. Jesus, though rejected, was made King, and He is ruling and reigning with His Father right now. But He is coming back! It doesn't matter that they did not want Him to be King, He is King and He will return. In much the same way, the world does not want to accept Jesus as Lord of this world. Why? It's just not "politically correct"! I love how verse 15 starts: "He was made king, however, and returned home." You know, it doesn't matter what the world thinks or what their opinion is; the fact is, Jesus has been crowned King by God the Father, and He is coming back to set up His Kingdom. As the Bible says, every knee will bow. It will not be a day for opinions, let me assure you! In the light of the times and biblical prophecy, that day is coming soon!

Jesus continued with the story, telling the disciples that the master returned and called together the servants and asked them, "How has my kingdom fared while I was away? What have you done with the money I gave to you, and in specific, what have you gained?"

What is going on here?

Is this a time of accountability?

Yes, it is. For the Master, Jesus, is asking upon His return, "How has My Kingdom fared with those things that I gave to you to take care of for Me while I was away?" Hey now, if you have taken a carefree and irresponsible attitude toward the handling of the Master's money, this is heavy Scripture! Now remember, salvation, finances, and the Kingdom were the topics of discussion at this dinner meeting at Zacchaeus' house. Jesus not only informed them that the time to set up the Kingdom was not near and that there was work to be done, but also that there would be a time of accounting regarding the use and growth of the assets of His earthly Kingdom.

Don't argue with *me* about this; remember, these words are in red! You have to take it up with Jesus.

Let's go on...

The servants came in to report. The first servant reported a growth of 1,000 percent. (I think this guy must now work for a major mutual fund company in the aggressive growth category.) The master's mina had earned ten more! The master was pleased and gave the servant a reward. The servant was trustworthy in a small matter; consequently, he was put in charge of 10 cities in the kingdom.

I guess we might call him the President!

Then in came number 2, a more conservative money manager with only a 500 percent return. He probably was heavily involved in bonds in an up market, but hey, I'll take a 500 percent return any day, and so did this master! He rewarded this servant with charge over 5 cities.

This guy we'll call the Governor!

Notice, the master rewarded responsibility according to the ability shown. There is a principle being taught here about how to increase our wealth. In order to increase our blessing and be charged with more responsibility, we must increase our ability to do things God's way. God rewards faithfulness in small things by increasing our blessings. Poverty theologians, if you are out there, this blows your theology right out the window!

Shhh! Jesus talking here!

The master knew that if his directions had been followed, the result would be one of success. Invest! Put the money to work until I come back! The new president and new governor had proven the master right!

Then in walked number 3. The master asked, "Servant, how has my kingdom fared with those things I gave you to take care of for me while I was away?"

This servant we will call "Hank" (that's short for Brother Hanky). Hank pulled a hanky out of his pocket, cautiously unfolded it to reveal the mina, and said, "Sir, here is your mina. I hid it so I would not lose it." Now I want you to catch his next three words...

"I...was...afraid!"

Fear—the beast that consumes you! Fear—the tool of the devil! You know fear—*False Evidence Appearing Real!* That which we fear, we also empower! The Bible tells us that the enemy has no power over us. All he can do is say, "Boo!" All he can do is speak fearful thoughts at us, which have power in our lives only if we listen to them and empower them ourselves. Hank refused to trust the master's directions to put the money to work and chose not to act as instructed, for fear of failure. Fear of losing the money and reaping the repercussions of the master's disapproval prevented Brother Hanky from experiencing the success the master knew would come as a fruit of *obedience.* (Ah, there's that word again!) Fears that cause disbelief are enemies to spiritual joys! They prevent us from achieving what the Master intended and from attaining the purpose in our lives for which we have been called. (We will talk more about this subject in Chapter 17, "The Ultimate Identity Theft.")

Success was lost! The master was displeased and told Brother Hanky that he was judged by his own words. Brother Hanky feared the judgment of the master and did not do as he was told because he was afraid of losing the mina. Ironically, it was the use of human reasoning instead of obedience that caused this servant to be punished. The master held him accountable and scolded him for his slothfulness, because he neglected to even deposit the money with the banker "so that when I came back, I could have collected it with interest" (verse 23).

The master then ordered those around him to take the mina from him and give it to the one with 10 minas! The people were amazed. "Why, Lord?" they asked. "He doesn't need anymore. He already has 10 and now he's the Prez!"

The master had already lost money by entrusting it to the unfaithful servant, so he then gave it to his best money manager to try to make up the loss! He told them that He would give more to those who had been successful in managing his affairs, but he would not entrust more to those who had little success. Hey, doesn't the financial world fire poor money managers and give the money to new managers who have a successful track record? So does our Master. If you don't think so, check the red words again.

Think of this: I as a financial advisor manage investment portfolios. Imagine that I manage your investments. Year after year, you come in to see me and I confess that I have not been diligent with your money. If I say, "I am so sorry. I have been so busy, and I just have not had time to review and put any effort into your portfolio. I have just been winging it as far as the decisions I have made, but I will do better next year"; do you think you would find a new money manager? You bet you would!

Well, according to Jesus, so did this master!

"Hey, wait a minute, Buck!" you say. "That's not my Lord. My Lord provides for us, loves us, and wants to bless us with prosperity. That is the way I understand Him!"

Yes, that is the way I understand Him too. He does want to bless us, and He wants us to succeed. That is why He has given us instructions in His Word on how to succeed—over 2,350 verses! Success is the fruit of obedience to His financial instructions. Have you read them? Do you know them? Or have you squandered or buried your educational opportunities to learn to be the Master's manager of accounts (steward)? Fortunately, the difference with our Master is that He always gives us a chance to restore ourselves. Poor money managers can become good money managers. Stingy ones can become generous.

If you still don't buy this, then let's read some other red words in Luke. Look up Luke 16:11 in your Financial Manuals: "So if you have not been trustworthy in handling worldly wealth, who will trust you with true riches?" (NIV) Jesus speaking again here, not Buck!

The parable ends here with the judgment of those who had not accepted the King's lordship. This speaks of the judgment of unbelievers, those who have not made Jesus Lord of their lives, which occurs when the Lord sets up His Kingdom! If you are not sure whether or not you will be part of that judgment, we will talk more about this subject in Chapter 18 and you can be sure of so great a salvation that the Lord Jesus provides.

The parable ends, but what is missing?

Listen, this is BIG!

Remember, there were ten servants to whom the master gave each a mina. Three had their time of accounting. But what about the other seven? What happened to them? How were they found faithful?

We don't know, because the jury is still out on them!

Listen, this is important! *Seven* is the number used throughout Scripture by God to signify fulfillment or completeness; in essence, all things being done and in order. Those seven servants represent us—all the servants of the Master who have yet to experience their time of accounting. They represent those servants who the Lord has yet to ask, "While I was away, how has My Kingdom fared with those things I have given to you?"

All His servants will ultimately be held accountable, and we will rule and reign with Him according to our faithfulness, which according to Jesus includes our financial faithfulness.

Unfortunately, the Church of Jesus Christ is presently full of Brother Hankies!

I too have been a Brother Hanky.

Perhaps you have just declared yourself a Brother Hanky!

You may have been unfaithful with your mina because you have been afraid to step out in faith and do things the way the Master has instructed you. Or you may not handle your financial responsibilities correctly because you don't know how, or have not had the discipline to do so. You may have never read His instructions and applied biblical principles to the handling of your finances. The teaching of the Church has neglected this major subject down through the ages, which is why so many Christians have stepped out of God's plan.

The good news is that it does not have to remain that way. We now have the tools available to the Church so that they can teach the steward how to be faithful to the Master's instructions.

God is a God of restoration and even a Brother Hanky can still become the Prez in Christ's Kingdom!

Christ has transformed other areas of your life; have you also allowed Him in your checkbook?

Remember, God doesn't need your money, it's already His. What He needs is your obedience! This is why finance and prosperity are such divisive issues within the church. Obedience in financial matters is an area with which most people have difficulty. However, I have found in my own life that when I am obedient in the areas of finances and giving and tithing, it makes being obedient easier in other areas of my life as well. If you can learn to do what the Master asks in the area of finances, even when it is scary and does not make much human sense, you will find that your faith will increase in all areas of your life. It did in mine, as well as many others who have testified to a changed life as a result of obedience to the Word in their finances.

I recall sitting at the breakfast table with a well-known mighty man of God who had experienced much fruit in His ministry, which spanned over 50 years and showed no sign of letting up. He had been widely criticized over the years because of his strong emphasis on paying the tithe and giving sacrificially to the work of the Lord. In fact, at one time in my life, I myself even wondered what his intentions were, but I noticed that he walked in blessings. In the light of the ministry God had called me to, I became very bold as I took advantage of the opportunity to gain a direct answer from him as to why this was a regular message of his ministry. He drew close to me, looked me straight in the eye, and gave me an eye-opening answer that seemed to go straight to my soul; and impacted me greatly as the Holy Spirit confirmed it in my spirit.

He told me that while the giving of others enabled him to continue his ministry, it was not his main reason for preaching about tithing and financial sacrifice, for he had learned to depend on God for his provision, not on "persuading stubborn people." He said only the Holy Spirit can persuade people in this area. He also stated that he wanted others to learn as he had learned to become faithful in the area of finances, "for then, Buck," he continued as he sat back with enthusiasm and raised his voice as he waved his arms, "if they can become faithful in their finances, they will grow in faith and become faithful in all areas of their walk with Christ." He continued to explain that if someone had not strongly impressed him to give out of obedience and out of his need, he would have never learned how to receive God's blessings not only in finances but in every area of his life. Obedience in finances allowed him to break out into the fruitful ministry he has enjoyed for many years. "Now why would I not want that for all of God's people?" he asked. Yet still today, Christians make fun of and criticize him because they still do not get it.

The truth is...

Christ has ordered us to use our finances in preparation for the coming Kingdom. We prepare by becoming financially faithful in the management and giving of our, *whoops*, excuse me, *His* money. This not only concerns the elimination of debt, both individually and corporately within the Church, but also through proper financial planning and estate planning. You can be doing well with your investments and debt management but still be a Brother Hanky if you are not planting seeds from those investments into the Kingdom of God, or if you are investing and managing that money contrary to biblical principles.

We are talking about more than the tithe here! We as His money managers must do things that advance Christ's Kingdom. How does a Christian invest in the Kingdom? He or she does so by managing money wisely and by blessing ministries through distributing the Master's money to other servants of the Master who have a need.

Kingdom work and Kingdom investing will bring about that great and final Kingdom of our Lord!

Praise God! Get excited about this!

The truth is...

The Master is coming back, and He has ordered us to be faithful, not just with the 10 percent, but with the 90 percent. He wants us to trust Him at His word and to use faith in the use of His money in order to advance the Kingdom!

We have a clear mandate not just here in Luke 19 but throughout all Scripture. Paul, in Second Corinthians chapter 9, urges the believers to prepare gifts to ministries in advance, to save, to invest, and to stock up wealth so they can fill a need when they see it. Paul also encourages the believers in Second Corinthians 12:14 and First Timothy 5:8, to save for their family's security and future. We are to provide for ourselves, our family, and give out of our surplus to the Kingdom. We are not to hoard money. Jesus teaches us this in Luke 12:13-21, the Parable of the Rich Fool; and First Timothy 6:9-11 warns against the accumulation of wealth for the wrong reasons.

As a financial advisor, I know there are many Christians who suffer from what I call the "Stingy Steward Syndrome" and qualify as a Brother Hanky under this category. When the Master tells this steward to send some of His assets to another steward to fill a need, he ignores the call. He does not want to seed into the Kingdom because it might reduce his surplus or mess up his current portfolio. When the Spirit calls him to do something, he becomes fearful! It is then that the enemy sneaks in and whispers that paralyzing question, "What if you need it?" Consequently, he does not give out of his surplus cheerfully and does not include ministries in his estate planning. This syndrome is probably more accurately called the "Fearful Steward Syndrome." This steward is afraid to take the Master at His word and has a difficult time believing that if he obeys and seeds (gives) into the Master's Kingdom, He will respond to his obedience and multiply it in return.

God also calls ministries to seed into other ministries. However, ministries might use the provision to fulfill some "convenience" needs of their own, while another ministry's "necessity" needs remain unmet. Are we giving additional perks to our ministry leaders, redecorating facilities, or making purchases of "convenience" while brothers and sisters in Christ elsewhere are going without such things as food, clean water, and medical care? Maybe we should buy them a plane to fly in the needed supplies. I have personally experienced what $20 (buy medicine to save a life of a newborn), $50 (fund an evangelistic conference), and $400 (fund a full-time pastor for a year) can do in Africa.

When ministries talk to me about some plan to raise money for estate gifts or to use estate gifts, I always ask the question, "Is this a *necessity* or a *convenience?*" If it is a convenience, should we consider seeding our money first? We know what happens to seeds, don't we? They grow! I am talking about getting needs of the Body at large met, and eventually, also meeting those conveniences. I am talking about turning the wealth of the world back into the hands of God's people.

Consider this ministry, leaders and stewards…

The more we "seed," the more wealth of the world the Lord must draw on to bring us our harvest. He must "cash in" on the world's wealth, which means that more wealth will be transferred into the hands of God's people, fulfilling Deuteronomy 8:18 and Proverbs 13:22b.

Read those last two sentences again! We will visit this more in the last chapter of the book.

How about you? Do you have any money that is not doing anything to advance the Kingdom? I was once consulted by a church that had received a sizeable endowment ten years earlier, which had grown substantially since then. Their problem: They had never used that money for anything, because they did not need any of it to support the regular ministry of the church.

How sad!

The Master's money had been rolled up in a cloth and had never been invested in the Kingdom! The Scriptures have more to say on this subject, and we will continue to look at what the Bible has to say.

Whenever I am asked my opinion on an issue where God's Word is already clear, I usually respond that I do not have an opinion on that subject. When God is clear on an issue, I am not entitled to an opinion. This issue of finances and the Christian is clear. In Titus 2:9-10, Paul tells us how servants are to behave. And remember, we who name the name of

Christ are all God's servants, just as Christ was, His servant Son! My paraphrase of this passage puts it simply: "Don't talk back or steal, and show you can be trusted." When it comes to finances for the Christian, it's that obedience thing again! According to the Master, you and I do not have an opinion!

There are only two types of servants—obedient and disobedient ones. What category do you fit in?

Remember, there is no condemnation for Brother Hankies (see Rom. 12:1). God wants to shine the light of His Word on us to move us to action, not condemn us. The Lord loves those He chastises. Sometimes God fans our flame by flaming our fanny!

Are you with me? Let's learn some more. Hold on to your hats if you are motivated to be declared a faithful steward. We are about to ride the crest of the wave of the Spirit as He moves us into becoming the financially faithful Church.

The revolution has begun!

CHAPTER 4

PARALYZED BY THE LIGHT

In speaking engagements and in private sessions, I am often asked the question: Why is a believer who is tithing and giving sacrificially, still suffering, experiencing a lack of necessities, or not able to meet his bills?

My usual reply to that question is:

If the person truly and sincerely is being obedient in tithing and giving, it is usually because there is still something our Lord wants that individual to learn about managing money. Although there may be other reasons, usually when time allows me to research their finances more thoroughly, I often find the same situation that needs correction.

Many people are receiving enough income to have their needs met, but are not now managing or have not in the past managed the provision wisely; usually because they don't know how, or do not want to put forth the effort to do so. Today, the Church of Jesus Christ has the educational resources available to help the believer learn to manage finances wisely; yet, according to surveys, 90 percent of churches still do not have a regular program to teach the steward how to truly be the Lord's "manager of accounts"—which is how Webster defines the word *steward*! This is why I have dedicated myself to the ministry of helping God's people become financially faithful.

There is also another reason that we will get into shortly.

Our churches today focus mainly on the giving and tithing part. The 10 percent, as we will discuss later, is infinitely important! *I said before that the failure of the steward to be obedient in the 10 percent area is most often due to how he or she handles the 90 percent.*

So many Christians have come to me with condemnation all over them because they know they are not obedient in this area, although they want to be. Things are so upside down that when they do get money, it goes to cover money already spent, and they are afraid to write a check for the tithe for fear it will bounce! Am I talking to anyone out there?

"How do you know this?" you ask. I know because I have spoken with many out there who are like that!

Church leaders, stewards—this should lead us into action! We want to tithe; we want to fill a need when we see it, but we can't. We've been paralyzed! We then go to church or turn on the radio or TV and hear a message about how we are robbing God by not tithing or giving generously and condemnation gets all over us! This too is another tool of the devil. *He will bring condemnation on the believer by shining the light of the Word on them.* The accuser says, "Look at you! You're a Christian and you're not tithing! Look at you, you're a Christian, and your finances are a mess! You are unworthy and not fit to do the Lord's work! Give up! You are lousy with money and you always will be. Don't even try! Whatever you do, don't let anyone know. Keep it to yourself. You will never get out of this hole!"

Just like a deer standing on a dark road can be paralyzed by an oncoming headlight, we too can have the light of the Word of God shine on us, yet be paralyzed with condemnation! Not only are we not giving, but we also have been taken out of any type of effective ministry. The enemy then says: "Mission accomplished!"

This type of light paralyzes us, but we have to recognize who is holding this light. It is not God, for He wants to restore us to His perfect will! His desire is to bring us to the light of obedience and then to restore us, not to paralyze us with condemnation. He wants to use the light of obedience to show us the way! He wants to move us to action! This is conviction from the Holy Spirit to motivate and move us to action, not condemnation that disables us.

Consider and memorize the following illustration, which I have used for many years, so you can understand the difference between condemnation and conviction and quickly recognize them. Condemnation and conviction are like cousins. What do we know about cousins? Sometimes they look alike, maybe even talk alike; but do they have the same father? No, cousins do not have the same father! Condemnation's father is the devil who wants to render us ineffective by paralyzing us. Conviction's father is the Holy Spirit who wants to move us to action so that we can be all that the Father has purposed us to be.

What then, in obedience to God's commands on giving, does it take to become financially faithful? Here are some other things that must be added to tithing and giving in order for the steward to be successful:

Faith: It takes faith—that step-out, overcoming, "I can do all things through Christ who strengthens me" kind of faith. When you let go of what is in your hand, God will let go of what is in His hand for you. Webster's Dictionary tells us that faith is a noun, but I maintain that the day we accept Christ as our Lord and Savior, it becomes a verb! Peter says to "prepare your minds for action"(1 Pet. 1:13). Paul tells us to "work out our salvation" (Phil. 2:12). Action! Do something that is evidence of your faith! Remember Zacchaeus? He did something with his money that was the evidence of his faith. *Faith is not only a possession; it is an activity!*

Effort: Here is the one that is most often neglected. In Luke chapter 19, the judgment and rebuke was for the servant who showed no effort in handling the master's money.

As I've said previously, I manage investment accounts. If year after year you come to me and I have not been diligent with your account, or if I consistently lose money in your portfolio and I do not carry out your instructions, would you find a new money manager? You bet you would! According to Jesus in Luke chapter 19, so also will the Master find a new steward to handle His money! If we do not *discipline* our flesh to do what it should, we will not be successful. I'm talking about the the First Corinthians 9:27 kind of discipline—one that takes effort!

Education: The fact is, most of us have never learned how to manage the Master's money. What we know we have been taught by the world. Remember that there are over 2,350 verses in the Bible to tell us how to handle money and possessions, and even many of our church leaders do not even know what the Bible has to say. Fortunately, the educational resources are now available to the Church. Let's start using them. Remember church leaders, that when it comes to the people in the church...they don't know that they don't know!

Accountability: As I have said previously, the occasional sermon or church class or seminar is not the answer! Right afterward, as the motivation wanes, things go back to as they were! I have been there and done that for too long without the results that I am now seeing in my endeavors. We need accountability to be part of the change process. The Crown Financial Ministries small group study is one of the best ways to accomplish this. Through this program, people are helped, loved, and held accountable as they put forth the effort to become financially faithful.

In summary, when most people get past the faith part and get into the effort part, they often lack the discipline or the ability to go all the way in becoming financially faithful. Most churches lack the discipline and the effort, as well as the ability, to help their people become financially faithful. Accountability to group members is the key!

We may as well get used to accountability in finances, for one day the Master is coming back, and He will ask us, "How has My Kingdom fared with those things that I have given to you?" (See Luke 19.)

Ministries are suffering paralysis today because they either lack the money or face a deficit of manpower or womanpower. Instead of tapping into their God-given power, Christian men and women have been paralyzed by fear! The corporate church can be paralyzed by debt and/or need as well. I guarantee you that finances are at the root of most problem issues corporately and individually.

Nine out of ten couples or individuals I have counseled with have told me they have not discussed their financial situations with their pastor, and many pastors are in the dark on this subject. I am amazed at the lukewarm or cold response financial ministries get from pastors. Many just do not see it or in some cases do not want to. If you or your church show symptoms of paralysis, you may need to focus on the subject of finances, and you may need some help doing it! Many programs and methods have been tried, but failed. Get help from those who have had success; do not try it alone. So much time has been lost with the "do it myself," "I'll write my own program" church leader. When God calls us to financial faithfulness, we must show effort as well as faith if we are to break the financial paralysis in our life and in the ministry of the Church!

I have always said that what the corporate church is experiencing is usually a reflection of what is happening in the individual lives of the people who make up that body. Think about that for a minute. What is going on in your church body? Most likely, the same things are happening at home.

God is calling His people to financial faithfulness; sadly, our refusal to act is paralyzing us! If you are still not convinced, keep on reading.

CHAPTER 5

THE FINANCIAL STATE OF THE CHURCH

ADDRESS

There is a time of the year, usually in January, that we hear our elected politicians and corporate heads give an annual report on the state of the country, state, or organization they represent. This address includes the status of its economy. If we were to complete an annual report for the Church, and I was to write it, I believe it would read something like this:

The American Economy is the strongest it has ever been. Inflation is low, and though the stock market has had its ups and downs lately, investments have performed well over the past several years. Many of God's people have benefited from the economy, but like many Americans, God's people have also struggled with money problems. Many of God's people are suffering not only because of willful disobedience to God's principles, but many unknowingly are violating God's financial principles. Let me summarize some areas that are deeply affecting the Church.

GIVING

Giving a percentage of income has declined almost every year for the past 26 years. The average Christian gives 2.5 percent of his income to the church, and over 50 percent of all giving in the church is given by those who are age 65 or older. Our Lord has instructed us in His Word that 10 percent of our income must be given in order for us to become part of God's blessing cycle. (See Malachi 3:8-12 and First Timothy 6:18.)

DEBT

Consumer debt is increasing in America at a rate of $1,000 per second. Financial difficulties in the home are blamed for 56 percent of all divorces. In my counseling of Christians, I have found that they, like most Americans, have an average credit card debt of $10,000 to $20,000 with payments of $300 to $400 per month. That is $300 to $400 per month that could be directed toward evangelism instead of to some bank. It is no wonder with this type of debt spiraling out of control that 1 in 69 families in your church this year will be forced to declare bankruptcy. Many churches are not debt free and are a servant to the lender. (See Proverbs 22:7.)

Gambling

Yes! Gambling is surfacing in the Christian community. The development of state lotteries has made the get-rich-quick lure of the devil more tempting to the Christian. In surveys, questionnaires, and my own personal experience in counseling, I find that many Christians will spend $100 to $250 per year on lottery tickets when buying their gas and milk. "It's just so convenient," and "What's a buck or five anyway? Hey, if I win, I'll give a gift to the church!" Contrast this to the average of $20 spent per year by church members on missions. (See Proverbs. 28:22 and First Timothy 6:9-10.)

Savings

Savings are virtually nonexistent in most Christian homes today. In God's Word, we are told to save, yet we violate this principle. The savings rate in America is at its lowest in 59 years, and this lack of savings creates financial instability. When faced with a crisis, the average Christian has no alternative but to take on new debt. (See Proverbs 21:20.)

Estate Planning

Many Christians are woefully unprepared for the settlement of their estates. Many have only a will, which is just the beginning, and few have addressed the estate and retirement plan tax issues or have set up gifts from their estates to bless ministries committed to advance the cause of Christ. It is estimated, and my experience bears it out, that only 5 to 10 percent of Christians have adequately prepared their estate plans and have included ministries in their estate gifts.

Unfortunately, I see little difference in the way most Christians handle their finances compared with the way secular society does. My biggest frustration is that pastors and church leaders do not catch the vision of what could happen if a program would be implemented in their church. We must begin now to train younger Christians how to handle money God's way and to teach older Christians to plan their estates with ministries in mind. In doing this, the Church will receive adequate funding to do the work it has been called to do.

END OF REPORT

It is not a very encouraging report, is it? Unfortunately, it is the truth. I am sure it will not receive a rousing hand of applause from the leadership of the Body of Christ. Hopefully, it will cause them to repent and move to better equip the Body to handle their finances according to the great Financial Manual, the Word of God.

What are the problems facing the steward, the Master's manager of accounts today? Let us take time to look at the individual problem areas the Christian steward is facing and see where and how the enemy has set up camp in the financial lives of God's children.

PART 2

CHALLENGES FACING
THE REVOLUTIONIST

CHAPTER 6

BUDGETING—THE FAMOUS "B" WORD

Budgeting—yes, this is the number 1 financial challenge for a reason. This is the famous "B" word that everyone tries to avoid. A budget is that thing that many people want to develop but never seem to get done. Perhaps we should start teaching our young children when learning the alphabet that "A" is for accountability, "B" is for budget, "C" is for credit, "D" is for debt, and so on! Get them off on the right foot.

A budget is a financial road map that takes you from where you are to where you are going, and it is the most neglected thing in the Christian's financial plan. The main reason is that very few people really understand how to develop a budget or what it even is! Most people think that if they are monitoring their income and their outgo, they have a budget. Not so! The only thing they have is a tracking device! Remember this thought that I have taught people for a number of years: *A budget is a traffic cop to tell your money where to go; it is not a tracking device to tell you where it went!*

No budget is ever successful unless it includes savings. If there are no savings, then the first time an emergency arises, the budget already becomes ineffective. So remember this thought as well: *A budget without savings is a budget waiting to blow up!* Christian financial resources listed in this book will provide you with guidelines to help you develop a budget. In the Crown Small Group Financial Study, one of the first things you do is develop a budget, and throughout the 12-week study, you fine-tune it. It takes about a year to develop a truly accurate budget as you record income and spending; and throughout your life, you will continue to fine-tune it and adjust it at least annually. Developing a budget is step one in achieving financial freedom.

One of the most difficult budgeting problems occurs when there is a fluctuating income in a family, and the paycheck is not always the same. This is usually a problem for people whose income is based on commissions or in the case of a family-owned business or sole proprietorship. The tendency is usually to spend money as it comes in; some months we are rich, and some months we are poor. This type of problem also occurs with contractors who are paid on a job-by-job basis and may be affected by seasonal demand.

People with fluctuating incomes need to budget for survival, setting aside money for the off season or for those times when things are just not happening and income falls off. Most contractors fail, not because their work is not good or because they cannot get work, but because they have no savings.

The best approach is to take your annual income from the year before and divide it by 12 to determine a monthly budget figure. If business is increasing, and income is higher this year, the surplus should be used for debt reduction and savings. This will free up more income as debt is retired and develop a cushion on which to build or to fall back on if necessary. Remember what a budget is without savings! (KABOOM!)

If you have difficulty in developing a budget, there are written resources available to assist you, usually at your Christian bookstore. Credit counseling agencies also will assist, but my experience with them is that they do not always understand the Christian or God's commands. They will immediately tell the Christian to stop giving while working his way out. This is good worldly wisdom, but it takes the Christian out of God's blessing cycle. I suggest that you seek the counsel of a Christian budget counselor. Crown Financial Ministries has trained budget counselors all over the country, and a call to them or a visit to their website will refer you to a trained counselor in your area.

Most importantly, the husband and wife should both be involved in the development of a budget, which is biblical. Whereas, if there is an uninvolved partner, he or she will be operating in the dark and may not be committed to it. It is difficult to be successful if there is not a commitment on the part of both spouses.

I often hear the comment, "Buck, my finances are so far out of whack, I cannot even develop a budget." That is the very reason they are "out of whack" in the first place, and only by working a plan will they get back into "whack." *Disorganization does not breed organization; it breeds more disorganization. Organization breeds organization and helps you to see things more clearly and to map your progress.* Budget, and then follow it as best as you can, even if it does not make any sense. Why? Because while starting to get things organized, God will also honor your obedience.

Without a budget, it is difficult to manage money properly, to develop an investment program, or to tithe and give properly. It also creates misunderstandings between marriage and business partners.

CHAPTER 7

DEBT—THE CHURCH'S ENEMY

D ebt is the enemy of the Church, both individually and corporately. It is a tool of the enemy to keep the believer's focus on serving money rather than on serving God. It takes the believer out of ministry and puts him or her into bondage. Corporately, the debt of a church has been known to break unity within that body of believers.

Those of us who have incurred debt know what it means when Proverbs 22:7 says, "The rich rule over the poor, and the borrower is servant to the lender." Is it any wonder we have problems in America? The philosophy of using OPM (other peoples' money) prevails in America, and Christians have been taught that it is the way to get what they need and want. Many of us get that "plastic" look on our face when we see something we want but don't have the money to buy it. What happens? Yep, out comes the credit card!

I remember when President Carter suggested that Americans cease using their credit cards and cut them up to help eliminate spiraling consumer debt and curb inflation.

Wow, it's a wonder they didn't impeach him! How un-American!

Hey, I say we need to *Discover* an *American Express* to financial freedom so that we don't end up with a permanent *Visa* in the land of debt. We need to *Master* the *Card*, not let the card be our master. The U.S. economy is built on debt and is presently a house of cards waiting to collapse. Need it take the Church with it if it does? No, and again I say, "No!" It is very common for me to meet a Christian couple with $20,000 to $30,000 in credit card debt. The unbelievable statistic according to Crown is that 1 in 69 families within the Church declares bankruptcy each year. Christians want to give to ministries but are in such bondage to debt they cannot!

We hear messages about God's provision and about taking authority over our finances, but while it is imperative to look to God as our provider and to claim our God-given authority over our finances, it is also imperative to employ some practical commonsense steps to make that happen.

Good stewards need tools!

If you are in debt, you need to establish a plan to get yourself out of debt, and sacrifices will need to be made. Your goal in reducing debt should be to develop equity and build surplus in order to become a more effective minister of the gospel. Here are some steps you can employ to get out of debt, and to get into what I call "God's blessing cycle."

1. **Tithing:** Start tithing (yes, even if you do not have enough money to pay bills)! You have to get yourself into God's blessing cycle. It's that obedience thing again! God promises to multiply our giving back to us. Remember that anything multiplied by zero is still zero! So begin to tithe.

2. **Budget:** Here it is again. Establish that budget and fine-tune it! Don't just track your money; give it some direction. When you want to put out a fire, you must direct the hose at the source of the fire. You don't spray the water around in a haphazard way and hope the fire goes out. In the same way, you must direct that stream of income so that it is effective. Your financial fire hose is your budget. If you don't know how to develop one, get some help from a trusted friend or advisor. There are also a number of books in your Christian bookstore that will help you. Best yet, get involved in a Crown Small Group Financial Study. Remember that a budget without savings is a budget waiting to blow up! (Yes, I do repeat things; I want you to get it!) You must have savings factored in for it to be a real budget.

"Wait a minute! Tithe and save before bills? What is this guy talking about?" I hear some of you saying at this point. You think I have flipped my lid, don't you? Well if you do, let me ask you this, "How did you get into this mess anyway?"

Sorry about the interruption here, but I had to address some of my readers at this point. Let us go on...

3. **Emergency Contingency Fund:** You must save while getting out of debt to keep from going further into debt when an emergency arises. Many people who develop a debt reduction program forget this important part. Why is this so important? Whenever I ask clients who do not have an emergency contingency fund how they would handle an emergency, they get a very "plastic" look on their faces and look to get a *Visa* to a less threatening place. They are appalled to *Discover* that their own answer to an emergency need is to take on more debt. (Are you getting my point?) The emergency contingency fund is all-important in maintaining financial freedom and should be the core of any money management program.

4. **Set Priorities:** Remember that I said in order to get out of debt some sacrifices must be made? Can you cut back or even cut out some things until debt is paid down? Keep a record of personal expenditures in a small notebook for at least 30 days (husband and wife both keep one). It can be a real eye-opener! You will be surprised how much money "leaks" out of your pocket and how much you spend on incidentals that you might be able to cut back.

5. **Use Your Authority:** If you are struggling with debt, you must above all remember who you are in Christ—the child of a King, joint heirs with Christ, with power of attorney to use Jesus' name in taking authority over your finances. The enemy likes to attack us in this area and send condemnation reigning down on us. Call on your wealthy Father to help you. He owns the cattle on a thousand hills (see Ps. 50:10), and He will slay one for you if you are faithful, for He is faithful! (see 1 Cor. 1:9 and Heb. 10:23). Remember, however, that you must be walking in obedience to use your authority.

Here are some points to remember when it comes to debt.

1. Paying debt is an investment.

2. The emergency contingency fund is all-important in maintaining financial freedom.

3. A debt reduction program requires sacrifices.

4. There is no such thing as a budget without savings.

5. A general rule of thumb: Living within your income leads to financial freedom and a higher lifestyle!

6. You must tithe and plant a seed faith gift in order to put yourself into God's blessing cycle. It is not a formula; it is obedience.

7. You must use the power of attorney, the authority to use Christ's name in taking authority over your finances. Don't forget you are a King's kid!

CHAPTER 8

CREDIT AND CREDIT PROBLEMS

The use of credit is usually what leads to the problem area of debt. As Christians, we need to follow some scriptural guidelines. Now I must admit that this is often an uncomfortable area to address because we have learned that credit is the American way! We have learned to borrow to purchase something, instead of save for something. But…this has been the American way only in modern times. Most of our forefathers believed in paying off all debts on payday! My grandparents never had a credit card; it just was not available! But today, the fact is that personal consumer debt is rising at a rate of $1,000 per second, and most American families are just a few months from bankruptcy. According to U.S. government figures, consumer debt in America rose 50 percent from 1995 to 2000 and business debt rose 60 percent! This is especially interesting when you compare these statistics to the fact that during the same period income rose only 4 percent.

Yes, we have learned to buy now and pay later in installments! Even our churches are building on credit. We will talk more about the subject of church debt in a later chapter.

We have many people with the appearance of wealth, but what we are actually seeing is what I call "cash flow wealth." We have the "stuff" that makes us appear wealthy, but it is encumbered with debt that we are paying off with our income…sometimes just barely. More than one pastor has said to me that they are not only surprised as to how many of their people are in financial bondage, but *who* they are as well! Sometimes it is that member who seems the most affluent and secure.

What are some of the contributing factors to credit problems?

Outgo Exceeds Income

This is the obvious one. Easy credit makes this possible, and debt is accumulated ahead of an increasing income. Your cash flow can allow you to get further into debt than you realistically can support, and then all of a sudden it all catches up—usually because you do not have a working budget. (There is that word again!)

BORROWING CYCLE

In an effort to get ahead, we consolidate or borrow for purchases at expensive rates, and consequently, debt accumulates. People often take out second mortgages or home equity loans to pay off credit cards (taking unsecured debt and securing it with your home—why do we do that?) Usually what happens is that, again, there is no budget, no discipline; hence, up go the credit card balances again.

THE SECOND INCOME

This gets people into trouble? Yep, it does! Generally people go out and get a second income or the wife will get a job to help out in making up a shortfall, but often in short order, people soon spend up to their income. They neglect to use the extra income to pay debt only, or they forget to take into account some other considerations like:

1. A possible change in income tax bracket, raising the tax payout of the family.

2. Additional expenses due to the new job. Baby-sitting or day care costs, transportation costs, and costs for an appropriate wardrobe can quickly eat up the increase in income.

Thoroughly investigate whether or not there is a real benefit to a second income and whether the benefits outweigh the liabilities.

THE DREAM HOUSE

Here is a big mistake often made by young couples. They buy too much house too early and then become a slave to their new home. Or they may take on that handyman special and get in over their heads trying to make that house a home. Those of us who saw the movie "The Money Pit" know what I am talking about. I have counseled with people who got in way over their heads because they charged the repairs to their credit card and ended up not only with a mortgage but buried in credit card debt at high interest. I was a real estate broker for years, and during that time I heard many realtors close a deal by using the phrase, "Let your income grow into it!" Send that broker packing! That is not wisdom by any means and definitely not biblical. It is an enticing sales closing tool, but when heeded, it will turn your "dream house" into the "nightmare on Elm Street!"

POOR MONEY MANAGEMENT/HAPHAZARD SPENDING

Here it is again—the failure to use a budget wisely! We often fail to plan to control our living expenses; hence, we spend money in a haphazard way. This is usually characterized by taking money budgeted for one thing to pay for another, impulse buying, or using that two checkbook system I talked about in Chapter 1. If you find yourself using a credit card to buy necessities like groceries and other regular budget items, you are in trouble and spending money in a haphazard fashion.

CHRISTMAS

Need I say much more than this? Christmas is the time we spread good cheer, and we spread our money all around. There is so much pressure financially on people at Christmas that it often is the beginning of a downturn in their financial condition. People do not budget for the holiday season; consequently, they then take money needed to pay bills and spend it on presents for family and friends. It is a big source of increasing credit card balances. The one good thing we can say about Ebenezer Scrooge is that he saved and saved. So when he decided to have a good Christmas, he had the money to do what he wanted! If you do not budget for Christmas, the ghost of Christmas past will definitely visit you around February! I do not think the Lord would have us celebrate His birth by stepping out of His will financially.

HOME EQUITY LOANS

Let us call them what they are—second mortgages! Lenders have developed euphemisms for second mortgages, but many should carry a label: "Caution, this loan may be hazardous to you financial health!" I can't tell you how many people tell me that they do not have a second mortgage on their home but later tell me they have a home equity loan...and it is often at high interest rates! The most common use of these loans is to pay off debt, usually credit cards. We take unsecured credit card debt and secure it with our home. This usually doesn't help the situation; often it defers the problem. I know of many people who get a home equity loan to pay off credit cards but then continue to run up their balances. Often they fall even further in debt.

CREDIT CARD PHILOSOPHY

The philosophy is well stated in the credit card advertisements: "Why wait when you can have it now!" (Is that what we teach our children?) The philosophy that has developed that "you are what you carry" is totally absurd! They want you to believe that people will be impressed by what card you carry. Upon graduation from high school, 18 year olds get all kinds of offers to sign up for credit cards. All they have to do is sign and return the application. Get this—they do not even have to prove that they have a source of income. Is it any wonder that the average college student today has a credit card balance of about $2,000?

As a college freshman, my son Ben and his roommate read a flyer that was circulating on campus offering a free sub to anyone who would visit a well-known fast-food place. *How could they give away so many subs?* Ben thought. Later that day, the two of them went to collect that free sub, and when they arrived, they found the place packed with other students waiting to receive their free sub as well. Ben and his roommate immediately noticed that the students were filling out paperwork—an application for a Visa Student Credit Card...one of those high interest specials! Ben, because he had been taught about credit, turned to his roommate and said, "I am not applying for a credit card just to get a three-dollar sub!"

They left, but they were the exceptions. Others did receive their sub, but they also received some things of which they were not aware. They received an inquiry on their credit record, an open credit account on their report, their name and address sold to merchants who will now contact them in an effort to make them use the card, and of course, a high interest credit card. I am sure that the president of this university would not have approved because I know him personally. I wonder what moms and dads would have said if they had seen their child filling out the application? Many parents most likely never told their children about this kind of trap because they themselves were not aware of it. Ben said that nothing on the flyer indicated the conditions of receiving the free sub, and that they were enticed there by false pretences. He was reminded of the account in Genesis of Jacob and Esau, where Esau gave up his birthright for a bowl of stew. God says in Deuteronomy 28 that His blessing on us is as a lender and not the borrower. Yet these students were volunteering to enter into a borrowing relationship just for a sub! They lacked understanding of what they were doing.

It is so unfortunate that seemingly the moment a child becomes an adult, the world is at his doorstep teaching him the credit card philosophy while our churches ignore the issue.

Credit card companies advertise pre-paid credit cards as "gifts for children." Even our young children are targeted. "Cool Shopping Barbie" is marketed to children three years of age and over. The doll has a credit card and a card swiper for the child to use when Barbie makes her purchases.

Let me ask church leaders and parents this question…

If our little children were playing on the church playground next to the highway and every so often one would run into the road and be hit by a car, do you think you would vote to put a fence up?

You bet you would! You'd probably do it before you allowed them to play there in the first place.

Well, every day, our children are growing up and running out into the road of financial disaster…*but we haven't put the fence up! The educational resources are available today to the church how to teach our children God's way of handling finances, yet we still haven't put the fence up!* When it comes to credit, how should the Christian use it? Here are some simple guidelines to follow:

1. *Never borrow money needlessly.* Many people borrow money rather than save money to get things they want. They use credit as an easy way out. Proverbs 22:7 is a verse the potential borrower should memorize. "The rich rule over the poor, and the borrower is servant to the lender." The original word for loan is "bond." The person is bound by a contract, a written bond to the lender. We still call loans to

corporations and municipalities, bonds. Loans are bonds! Read the verse again!

2. *Never sign surety (co-sign).* Before I knew this principle, I co-signed twice in my life. Guess how many times I got burned? Yep, twice! When a lending institution informs a potential borrower that a cosigner is needed, what they are really saying is that the borrower is not credit worthy and a poor risk, and the only way they will lend money to him is if he can get someone who is credit worthy to back him up. Car dealers often will ask for a cosigner, but I have found that this doesn't mean the cosigner is the second name on the paperwork. In many cases, the paperwork doesn't list the name of the original borrower anywhere. This is especially prominent in family cosigners. Let me address an often-asked question usually by a parent of a young adult child: Is cosigning a different matter for your own child? The answer—no! Teach the child how to save first, not how to borrow. If a need must be filled, the parent should borrow the money and require the child to make payments to them. Then you will know if they are paying on time. A cosigner usually does not find out that the borrower is behind in payments for at least 90 days. Proverbs 17:18 says, "A man lacking in judgment strikes hands in pledge and puts up security for his neighbor."

3. *Never consider debts as long term.* Seek to pay off debts quickly. In Nehemiah 5:1-5, the Jewish people mortgaged their property during a famine in order to get food and to pay taxes. As a result, they became enslaved to their own fellow countrymen. Nehemiah took action to assist these people in eliminating their debt because as Nehemiah said, they had been bought from slavery only to be brought back into slavery. Did God ever get you out of debt to see you go right back into it again?

4. *Never borrow for investments.* Many people have been caught in the trap of borrowing money to make a "sure" investment. But when the investment sours, they find themselves

in debt. In the securities world, this is referred to as invest-ing on "margin." Simply put, it is borrowing money from a brokerage to buy stock. If the value of the investment falls, you receive a "margin call." This means you have to come up with the money, which represents the difference between the value of the stock and the amount loaned. If you cannot or do not come up with the money, the stock is sold to pay the debt. It usually does not cover the whole loan and you are left with not only losing money on a stock but also a debt to repay. You do not have a say about the sale of the stock if you do not meet the margin call. This is bad stewardship. Run from these types of investments. The Master gave us a mina and told us to invest; He didn't tell us to go borrow one for him, using His assets as collateral, and invest it! We are to take what He has given us and start there.

In conclusion, let me address a growing trend in the Church. I used to practice it myself until the Lord showed me in such an obvious way that He did not like it. What if your employer or bank sent you a memo today that informed you that from now on, in order to process your income, they would deduct 3 percent of your income as a fee for this service? How would you feel? Think about it before you read on.

Believe it or not, hundreds of thousands of dollars a year, at a min-imum, given to the work of the Kingdom, is now being diverted to the credit card industry, the very industry responsible for much of the bondage affecting the giving of the Church. Ministries are even encour-aging it because it allows them to get money faster to meet cash flow shortages, which are due to the Christian community's inability to give because of the financial bondage. This is incredibly shortsighted. I have had Christians admit to me that their debt has increased since they began to use credit cards to do their giving, because the average person does not use credit cards responsibly. The fact is, on the average, for every $1,000 given by credit or check card to ministries, $30 goes to the credit card companies.

In addition, many people are motivated to give this way because it helps them accumulate points for air travel or other incentives provided by the credit card companies. Should this even be an issue? If so, should we deduct from our giving the value of the services or plane tickets we have received as a result of our giving? The IRS now asks us to reduce our gift by the amount of the value received from the ministry if the ministry sends something to us as a result of the gift. Does this also affect or reduce our heavenly, spiritual harvest?

Go ahead and talk amongst yourselves!

I once had a ministry share with me that this practice of accepting credit cards costs them over $200,000 annually. What could that money have done in the Kingdom? This practice is growing at such a phenomenal rate that we have got to put the brakes on; it's literally starting to snowball. I have even heard ministers encouraging people to put their gift on a credit card, "as a seed for the elimination of their credit card debt." The Spirit within me did a back flip when I heard this one. No matter how I stretch it, I cannot justify biblically the philosophy "give what you don't have, believing that the Lord will erase the debt you do have, for paying what you didn't have, for something or a service you may or may not have now!" I believe in seed faith for eliminating debt, but it must be something of value like the two mites that the widow gave! This got Jesus' attention! (see Mark 12:42-43 KJV).

We need to give sacrificially out of obedience for God's provision in our life. I believe that a person giving the last $20 in his checking account gets Jesus' attention more than charging $200 on his credit card because he has only $20 in his account! We can get so caught up in fund-raising sometimes that we lose sight of the whole picture on the biblical teaching regarding money and possessions. As I've previously said, we focus on giving and tithing so much that we neglect teaching what the Word says to help the Church become better stewards so that they will become better givers and tithers. We need to address the root cause of this problem. If we get hold of this concept, ministry leaders will spend less, little, or no time on fund-raising efforts. And what is it that ministry leaders get criticized most for? The answer: fund-raising!

Leaders and individuals do not understand what a problem credit card use is in society and how it affects the work of the Kingdom. When I share this fact with ministry leaders and individuals, I find that they most often are not even aware of this problem. Ministry leaders, please take the time to calculate what this practice costs the ministry, and then educate your givers regarding this practice.

God has provided every step of the way in my ministry efforts so far, and as I was instructed by the Spirit at the outset and according to His leading, I have never once asked for money! You see, He wanted to teach me something. What is it I am doing? I am educating people regarding biblical principles, and as they learn, they hear the Spirit and they give! Recently, I experienced a budget shortfall, and so, one morning as I was working around the house, I asked the Lord what to do. I knew He had a plan, and later when I went to the office, there was an unexpected check and a note from someone to whom the Spirit had spoken to about the need. The check was exactly the amount of the shortfall.

I say, calculate the need, then educate the stewards, and God will provide as He works in the hearts of His people. I believe that as we do this, ministry leaders will spend more time in ministering and less time and money in fund-raising. Most ministers of the gospel who I know love to minister and wish they did not have to spend so much time finding ways to fund the work.

Again, it's an obedience issue—many are not giving as they should because they lack the understanding of biblical principles in financial matters.

CHAPTER 9

MONEY MANAGEMENT

When I ask people about their money management program, most of them have no idea what I am talking about. God's Word calls us to be good "stewards" (see Luke 12:42 KJV), faithful and wise in our dealings. Webster defines a steward as a "manager," "a finance officer," or a "keeper of accounts." So as a manager of God's money, what management method do you use? Do you have a program, or do you "rob Peter to pay Paul"?

Oh, by the way, contrary to how it may sound, the "robbing Peter to pay Paul" method is not biblical. I would expect that Peter especially would have taken a real firm stand against this one!

Okay, so you don't know if you have a good management program. First of all, it may not be your fault, because you were never taught this subject in school. As we grew up, most of us were totally unprepared to handle finances, but praise God we don't have to stay that way!

In my opinion, schools should have a money management course for seniors. Thank the Lord, Crown Financial Ministries has developed a program for teens to be used under the authority of the local church. (Youth pastors—check it out!)

Let me offer a model for money management that successful money managers use. (Notice I said "successful" ones use it!)

This entire model is built around that incredibly important emergency contingency fund that I mentioned before. This account serves as both a storage tank and as a conduit. Consider the diagram on the next page.

Depending on your circumstances, the amount equal to three to six months of regular expenses should be maintained as a minimum balance in the management account, to be used only as an emergency reserve. The steady balance allows for income to be deposited into the account enabling the manager to draw off and deposit into the regular bill paying or checking account only what is needed for regular living expenses. All surplus money can remain in the management account and can be drawn off as needed.

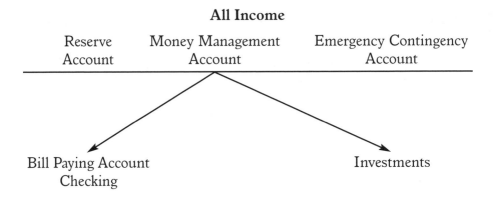

All Income

| Reserve Account | Money Management Account | Emergency Contingency Account |

Bill Paying Account Checking   Investments

Secondly, the account serves as a reserve account for those monies used to pay budgeted items that are paid less frequently than monthly (i.e., insurance, taxes, etc.). This money can be accumulated in the account and can earn dividends while waiting to be paid out.

Finally, the account serves as an investment-funding vehicle. When surplus money and earnings accumulate over the required balance (and if you use this method, it will), then money can be pushed off into higher yielding investments for your financial future.

The best type of account to be used as a management account is a money market account with check-writing privileges, managed by an investment or mutual fund company. It should also be linked electronically with your regular checking account. Usually, for ease of cash flow, I recommend that the account be established with a family of mutual funds with which you would like to make higher yielding investments.

How can you get started? The management/savings account can be started as part of a regularly scheduled monthly budget item. Current savings can be transferred to establish the account, or a tax refund might be used to begin the account. Investment companies usually require $500 to $2,500 or regular electronic monthly deposits to open these accounts.

And the Lord said; who then is the faithful and wise steward, whom his master will set over his household, to give them their portion of food at the proper time? Blessed is that servant whom his master when he comes will find so doing. Truly I say to you, he will set him over all his possessions (Luke 12:42-44 RSV).

This parable emphasizes the need to fulfill our obligations and not to fall into slothful ease or fail to do God's will. Budgeting, savings, tithing, debt reduction, and money management will reap the rewards of obedience.

This Scripture should spur us on to be obedient and manage wisely when these results are contrasted with the unfaithful steward of verse 47: "That servant...shall receive a severe beating."

I say, let's stop the beatings and start the blessings!

CHAPTER 10

HONESTY

It has been reported that 20 percent of the United States gross national product goes unreported each year and that employee theft is approaching the $1 billion-per-week mark. Most people admit to cheating on their income taxes at least once during their lifetime.

There is a real tendency, even on the part of Christians, to rationalize dishonest actions and behavior. Instead of declaring this action as theft, it is described as a "job perk." Instead of calling it "cheating on income taxes," it is justified as "what everyone does." Leviticus 19:11 says, "You shall not steal, nor deal falsely, nor lie to one another" (LB). We need to have a healthy fear of the Lord and of what He expects from us. The point here is that God cannot bless us if we are dishonest, no matter how well we handle our finances. One of the evidences of Zacchaeus' changed heart was that after years of dishonest dealings, he made restitution and began to deal honestly with others.

I remember when I was invited to speak at a church one Sunday morning—we had a great time in the Lord. The church had been conducting the Crown Financial Small Group study for awhile and things were really happening in the ministry. At the end of the services, my son Ben and I walked to the parking lot with a group of the church's leaders. We said our good-byes, and Ben and I jumped in the car, turned the key, and…nothing! Try again…nothing! Out we jumped, up went the hood, and after all our efforts failed, the men began to suggest, "Call Sam, call Sam" (not his real name). I asked who Sam was and learned that he was one of the men of the church who owned an auto repair business. The cell phones went to work, and before long, I was informed that Sam was on his way.

The elders explained to me that Sam had a very successful auto repair business that he used as an evangelistic outreach. In fact, that morning he had brought three of his customers to church. "Why, Sam is one of the best one-on-one evangelists we have ever seen. He has led many people to the Lord through his business and his powerful testimony." Sam was described as a feisty tough guy, a little rough around the edges, who had committed his life to the Lord after reading the Gideon Bible while imprisoned in a federal penitentiary. I learned that Sam "did time" for about 17 years for armed robbery and truck hijacking, most of those years in solitary confinement because of his temper and tough-guy attitude. Christ changed his life, and once he was released from jail, he moved to their city where no one knew his past to try and make a new start.

Needless to say, Ben and I were anxious to meet Sam. A few minutes later, a car came zipping into the parking lot and out popped a gruff, stocky man who went right to work on diagnosing the problem while in fun harassing the rest of us. After a few minutes, he announced that the alternator was the problem, but because it was Sunday, he could not get one until 7 A.M. the next morning. Consequently, Ben and I would have to spend the night. He informed me he would pick up an alternator on the way to the garage the next day and have me on the road by 9:00 A.M. We had no choice but to wait.

In the meantime, he started the car with a portable battery pack and told us to jump in. "Better let me drive, " he said, " 'cause we're gonna have to go through all the lights or we won't make it. I'll drive 'cause the cops all know me." *I'm sure they do,* I thought, as Ben jumped in the backseat and I took the passenger seat. And he was right—we did not stop for a single red light on the way to the shop.

As we proceeded to discuss the business of the car, this rough-and-tumble guy suddenly pointed his hand at me and said, "Ya know, I oughta put you out here along this road somewhere, after the grief you caused me." Surprised, I looked at Ben in the backseat who sat there looking at me with a smile on his face and his eyes twice as big as they normally are. I looked back at Sam and asked, "Why's that?" Sam continued, "Because of you—you and that study of yours—why...my wife and I did not sleep together for two weeks!" Again, I looked at Ben, and this time he looked like the farsighted farmer who just mistakenly tried to milk the bull! I was thankful at this moment that I knew of this man's commitment to Christ or I would have been concerned. "Why's that?" I asked...again.

"Well..." Sam continued, "you see, my business is partly a cash business and partly checks. I thought you only had to report what you got in checks as income to the IRS. Then after taking that study, I found out that God doesn't like that and that I was doing wrong. I didn't know...now I know...and ya know now what I gotta do? I gotta report the cash too!" Then he looked at me with a big mischievous smile and said, "Do you know how much money that is going to cost me? A lot! But let me tell you, it is not going to be as expensive as this repair job is going to be for you!" (I was glad he was smiling.)

He went on to explain that when he discovered he was being dishonest, he initially rebelled and then got into an argument with his wife that went on for days. He told me that once he got over the initial shock, he realized he needed to be obedient. "I didn't know I was doing wrong...now I do. And I have to change that!" I appreciated his honesty (especially with the bill the next morning) and his willingness to be obedient to the Word of God. Just like Zacchaeus, Sam displayed his faith through his personal management of his finances, despite how difficult it was. Believers are called to a higher standard. Paul says, "Each of you should look not only to your own interests, but also to the interests of others" (Phil. 2:4).

Daniel also provides a model for the Christian here. Describing Daniel, the Bible says, "They could find no ground of accusation or evidence of corruption, inasmuch as he was faithful, and no negligence or corruption was to be found in him" (Dan. 6:4 RSV). Believers should be known for their honesty and integrity in all matters. If your conscience is pricked...hey, that's healthy. Good change is often painful. Yes, many of us, including me, have fallen very short at times, but that is no reason why the future need be the same.

God is a God of restoration, and remember, despite your past, there is always a future with Christ!

CHAPTER *11*

TITHING AND GIVING

We have been made in God's image. Therefore, because God is a giving God, we, being in His likeness, must also become givers.

I mentioned before that by tithing and giving, we activate God's blessing cycle. God demands obedience in this area, and we must obey Him to become partakers of His blessing cycle. Christians in the United States alone have enough money to fund the work of every ministry in the world. Yet, they cannot give, because their finances are out of control. Think of the credit card debt and interest payments. If just these two categories were paid off, think of how much money could be freed up for the work of the Kingdom!

Let's consider Luke 6:38, where we find more "red words." Jesus said, "Give and it will be given to you. A good measure, pressed down, shaken together and running over, will be poured into your lap. For with the measure you use, it will be measured to you." What measure do you use in your giving?

The key to starting the blessing cycle is the first word in this verse: Give. If we give nothing, nothing is what we will receive. Anything multiplied by zero is still zero. We must tithe and give in order to get into the blessing cycle, even if we do not have enough money to pay our bills. Tithing is the obedience part! It is the foundation or the tilled garden in which seeds can be planted. It places us in a position where we can be blessed. We must then plant seeds (or offerings) in the tilled garden of the tithe if anything is to grow. We plant those seeds in the garden of the Kingdom and in the fertile soil of faithful ministries in order to reap a harvest from God. And just as God is the one who makes things grow in our earthly gardens, He is also the one who makes things grow in our

Kingdom garden. When we tithe in obedience, God promises to meet our needs. It is the seeds (offerings) we plant that God multiplies back to us by the same measure with which we sow. Our growth is in the seeds we plant!

The problem is that many Christians are often like birds...they eat the seed!

They may plant a seed, and then God blesses them as He promised to do. But instead of planting again from the harvest, they eat the new seed! God will not continue to give seed to the eater. He will provide for the eater's needs, but the eater will never grow anything! If he is ever to grow anything, or accumulate Deuteronomy 8:18 wealth, he must begin to plant seed from his provision, no matter how small. God wants to bless us, because He is interested in His Kingdom work being accomplished. He is interested in souls!

Many years ago, when Andrea and I were experiencing a special need, we first heard about planting seeds. I was initially skeptical, trying to figure out how this "seed faith" concept could work. We first heard of seed faith from Evangelist Oral Roberts, and after studying the Scriptures and confirming its scriptural basis, we decided to trust God and try it. I remember telling the Lord that I did not wish to be misled and that He was going to have to make it pretty obvious to me if this truly was of Him. It was a difficult time in our life and money was pretty tight.

One day, Andrea went off to the grocery store where she found another young woman from our church who was short of money and trying to figure out how she was going to get what she needed for her family with the money she had. Andrea thought about what food we had at home and that we could make do with it somehow. She then felt led to give the other woman the $25 she had as a seed in our time of need. She came home with no grocery bags and told me what she had done. I, being the great man of faith that I was at that time (not!) reminded her that it was the last cash we had until I got paid again. She knew that, but insisted that God would multiply our seed. Well, off I went to the office wondering what we were going to do, stopping on the way at the post office to check our mailbox.

In the box was an envelope from one of the financial institutions I had done business with as an advisor. Opening the envelope, I found a letter and a check. The letter stated that an error had been made in my contract payouts over a period of about a year. During an audit, the company realized that certain amounts of money were due and payable to me, but due to an accounting error, incorrect amounts had been sent to me. Enclosed was a check for $2,500 representing the underpayment of fees due to me. The check, so to speak, had God's fingerprints all over it and needless to say, it got my attention ($25...$2,500...hmmm).

The car turned right around and headed back home where I walked in the door to show Andrea that the Lord had already given us a harvest and multiplied that seed in return. That was the beginning of many times that God met our needs after we planted seeds, just like Oral had taught us. Since then, we have become believers in planting seeds, and we have seen God's provision not only in our lives but in others as well.

I want you to also have the opportunity to hear and learn this concept, just as we have learned it. So, I have asked my dear friend Richard Roberts and his father, Oral Roberts, to allow me to include *The Miracle of Seed Faith* by Oral Roberts in the Appendix of this book.

My role as an advisor has given me a front-row seat to so many illustrations of this blessing cycle and seed faith over the years. Let me share one that occurred just a few years ago. This story, which I wrote in my column, "The Buck Starts Here," illustrates seed faith giving. Seed faith giving is giving over and above our tithes to accomplish His purposes and to obtain that which we need.

THE BUCK STARTS HERE
A Biblical Perspective on Finances
By Buck Stephens

NOTE: Recently I have seen the Lord working miracles in the area of finances among His people who are willing to live by His principles. I thank God that He has used me and this column to bring about some wonderful things in the lives of His people. I wish to share one such story with you. It is just as incredible as the ones I am not able to include in this article.

Take a look at what can happen when obedience and faith are put into action!

AIN'T NO MONSTERS UNDER DAT BED!
An Incredible Story of "Seed Faith"

A few months ago, I took a Saturday and spent the day helping my son Ben organize and clean his room. The bulldozer was in gear and the dump truck was parked outside his window as we began to sort out his 11 years of "accumulated assets." I was especially amazed at the "treasures" which had been stored under the bed and how he would react with excitement at the rediscovery of these treasures hidden there in the past. Fortunately, I found nothing organic!

Recently, someone else did some treasure hunting under their bed and let me tell you what they found...!

In January, a pastor challenged his congregation to make a "seed faith pledge" to the church's building program, and a retired woman on a fixed income felt prompted by the Holy Spirit to do so. She prayed and felt led to pledge an amount per month that afterward she had no idea how to accomplish. Her present income was not adequately meeting her expenses. In fact, she was considering a move to a less expensive apartment! She committed it to the Lord and believed in His promises.

Later, while reading this column, the Spirit again prompted her to contact me and to receive counsel regarding her financial situation and the pledge she had made. We made an appointment and reviewed her budget, and it *seemed* apparent that she would need to make that move and that keeping the pledge was out of the question. Knowing God's faithfulness to His Word, I dug deeper. I asked questions about other assets and she informed me that her father had left her a relatively small amount of money in stocks. My interest quickened when I found that he had bought them for her when she was seven years old! I took the documentation and the stock certificates **that she had stored in a box under her bed,** back to my office in order to research them and come up with a valuation.

I began to make discoveries that were incredible! I discovered that the stocks had a market value beyond her wildest expectations and that if they were sold and the money placed into income funds, it would produce an increase in her monthly income **10 times the amount she had pledged!**

Now that's a tithe, isn't it? God had not only provided, but He also had orchestrated the transfer of ownership of these stocks from her father so that it would fall under some recent favorable tax law changes.

I called her and informed her of God's provision, and after the initial shock, what a time of rejoicing we had.

But wait, it doesn't stop there, it gets better!

The day came to sell the stocks, and the market surged. At the Spirit's prompting, I instructed the broker handling the trades to sell them all, and went back to my office. He called me a short time later on the intercom and asked if I would come to the desk to review some additional information he had received from the transfer agent. We discovered some options not exercised, and additional shares, which would substantially increase the amount of money she would receive.

I returned to my office where I was informed that my "seed faith" client was on the telephone. I answered the phone by saying, "Well, your Lord must really love you! She laughed and replied that He sure did, but that I might want to shoot her. She went on to tell me that she had gone and done it again and planted another seed faith gift in another ministry. She then realized that that seed had already been multiplied as I informed her of the additional increase she was about to receive.

Ya know, God can't be dead, 'cause He just went to the bank again!

I recently informed her of even some more additional money she would receive, and she asked, "Now, will that be it?" to which I replied, "Don't ask me, ask Him!"

Isn't it wonderful to know, that if we are faithful, He is faithful and His provision is waiting for us, **maybe even under the bed**! I was so inspired by this that I went home and looked under my bed. And ya know what I found?...Yep, "dust bunnies" and a missing sock!

You know, readers, when I wrote that article, I thought the story had ended, but it hadn't. About a year later when she came to meet with me to decide how we would pay the taxes on that money, she came with a "mystery paper" she had received in the mail. She did not have a clue what it was. I reviewed it and just started to chuckle with excitement! Somehow when we had located the shares of stock, some had not been transferred and escaped detection until then. God had reserved the amount she needed to pay the taxes and to pay for a planned trip to the Holy Land.

Isn't that amazing? Naw, that's God!

Wait, I'm not done yet.

A few months later, after she returned from Israel, she said she wanted to see me to talk with me about something. We met and she informed me that she had told no one of this, not even family, but she believed the Lord was calling her to do something. When she had been in Israel, she met a couple who ran a Christian school among the Palestinians, who told her of their need for teachers and aides at the school.

I thought she was going to ask me to help her make a financial gift to them, but no!

She went on to tell me that when she was 12 years old, her mother was quite ill and near death. She prayed and told God that if He would spare her mother, she would be a missionary for Him someday! Her mother survived and she never forgot that promise. However, she married and had a family, and the opportunity never came for her to make good on her promise. Now she was retired, children grown, and her husband had passed away some years before. Her question to me was:. Could you help me plan to travel to Israel and work at this school with this money?

Well, knock me over with a feather!

I made some preliminary plans with her, and we contacted the couple who ran the school to get more information. I encouraged her to talk with her pastor and then with his blessing, to talk with her family. Six months later we all stood at the airport saying good-bye to Iris James, who at the age of 70 fulfilled her 58-year-old promise and boarded that plane to be a missionary in Israel to Palestinian children. She served God in Ramallah, in the midst of the violence of 2000, all possible through faith and obedience.

Wow! Now say it backward! Wow!

Hey, what do you think God can do with you?

Take a break. Get a drink after that story and come on back. We have more to talk about!

CHAPTER *12*

TEACHING CHILDREN

You should tell them God's decisions, teach them God's laws and instructions, and show them how to conduct their lives (Exodus 18:20 NLT).

What in the world is going on?

There is so much chaos in the world with wars, rumors of wars, earthquakes, famines, floods, and ethnic group rising up against ethnic group. People are being led from the truth into the occult, new age, and cultic religions! All eyes are on Israel and the Middle East as they unknowingly play out with accuracy the prophetic Word of God. There is so much heartache, confusion, and a lack of understanding of what Jesus taught.

Hey, that's just like Jesus said it would be in Matthew chapter 24!

And Jesus answered and said to them, "See to it that no one misleads you. For many will come in My name, saying, 'I am the Christ,' and will mislead many. You will be hearing of wars and rumors of wars. See that you are not frightened, for those things must take place, but that is not yet the end. For nation will rise against nation, and kingdom against kingdom, and in various places there will be famines and earthquakes" (Matthew 24:4-7 NASU).

The word translated "nation" here is the Greek word *ethnos* from which we get the English word "ethnic." Perhaps Jesus had an advance copy of the *New York Times* from the 21st century…I don't think so! God knows the beginning from the end, and Jesus as the Son of God knew what was to come. He wished to prepare His people for this time yet to come. The task before the Church today is to teach the Word of God in all areas so that we will be prepared for that which is to come and so that we can be about His business. In contrast, so many of His people live this life as if it was the only life they were ever to live, preparing for education, careers, retirement, and so on while forgetting the eternal. Eternity is a long time, yet most of us spend little time preparing ourselves and our children for it. Indeed, many of us have not even made reservations for where we want to spend it. (And Heaven, according to Scripture, is for sure not the default decision. See Chapter 18 on how to make reservations.)

On March 3, 2005, *World Net Daily* (http://www.worldnetdaily.com/news/article.asp?ARTICLE_ID=43128) reported that the Barna research organization released a study that showed that Christians parent no differently than the "world." The study revealed that "born-again Christian parents are more likely to put an emphasis on seeing that their children get a good education than seeing them enter adulthood as followers of Christ." According to the article, George Barna who led the research reported on their website that "only three out of ten born-again parents included the salvation of their child in the list of critical parental emphases. Parents cannot force or ensure that their kids become followers of Christ, but for that emphasis to not be on the radar screen of most Christian parents is a significant reason why most Americans never embrace Jesus Christ as their Savior....The fact that most Christian parents overlook this critical responsibility is one of the biggest challenges to the Christian church." Barna continues, "You might expect that parents who are born-again Christians would take a different approach to raising their children than did parents who have not committed their life to Christ—but that was rarely the case."

Hmm...what's wrong with this picture?

We have become so fixated on the temporal while the eternal goes on hold. What was it that Jesus said in Mark 8:36? "For what shall it profit a man, if he shall gain the whole world, and lose his own soul?"(KJV). The fact that Sally or Johnny was class valedictorian or earned a college degree or achieved great things in the corporate world does not qualify them to enter the Kingdom of God! The most important thing at the end of our life is whether or not we know Jesus and have made Him Lord of our life.

The problem is that in this life, everyone wants a Savior, but not everyone wants a Lord! Everyone wants to escape hell, but not everyone wants to change his lifestyle!

We need to not only claim for ourselves and teach our children how to have a Savior but also how to have a Lord! To have a Lord means we do things His way! Many of us claim Him as Savior while still remaining lord of our own life! This is why we have the church full of Christians whose faith is a preference and not a commitment. Preferential Christians are 100 percent Christian until being a Christian conflicts with something they want to do; then they choose their own way. They are obedient until it becomes uncomfortable or causes them to deny something they do not want to give up. Whereas a committed Christian does what the Word of God says, even if he must deny himself.

Which one are you?

Now I know better than anyone (ask my wife!) that even committed Christians fall short in a lot of areas, but the difference is—it is not a routine thing. I am not trying to bring down the "cousin of condemnation" here whose father is the devil, like we talked about in Chapter 4; but rather a visit from the "cousin of conviction," whose father is the Holy Spirit, which is a good thing to happen to us once in awhile.

The Barna study also reported that most Christian parents take a "laissez-faire" attitude when it comes to what their children watch on television, listen to on the radio, or see at the theater.

I am amazed at the movies even adult Christians watch, an area in which many Christians are caught compromising. Andrea and I always told our children not to watch or listen to anything they would not listen to or watch with Jesus! Now that would clean up a lot of our acts!

The fact is that the movie and television industries are teaching our children that sex outside of marriage is okay, degradation of women is entertainment, filthy talk is acceptable and funny, and lifestyles that the Bible declares to be an abomination to God are "normal." The vast majority of people in television and movies laugh at the "religious right" (I prefer the phrase "delivered and biblical") and even openly mock and ridicule us at their self-glorifying events. I even once heard a well-known actor using a Billy Graham-type voice mockingly say on television that those "born againers don't like what is in the movies, but they keep coming!" Hmm…that should tell us a lot!

Andrea and I enjoy a good movie that does not offend our Lord, and we admit they are difficult to find. We are amazed sometimes at the movies and television shows that other Christians tell us they have seen and enjoyed. They are often movies or shows with explicit sexual and/or violent content, and these Jesus-loving people are not the least bit ashamed. Jesus, I believe, would have walked out while they stayed for the whole thing. When I was a child, it was considered sinful to go to the movies, and at that time the movies were not that bad. The church at large at that time boycotted the movies, not because of the movies themselves but because of the lifestyles of those associated with the motion picture industry. While that restriction, I believe, was taken too far (I remember going to see Charlton Heston in the Ten Commandments with my mother and feeling guilty), the pendulum has now swung too far the other way, and permissiveness (and numbness) has invaded the Church in this area.

Listen to me, our concern here is for our children as we allow them to watch and become accustomed to immoral behavior and think of it as normal. Many of us simply want to avoid the confrontation. But ignoring these things is like ignoring a small fire in the kitchen because it will probably burn itself out! You would not do that! Why? You know it will continue to burn and spread and consume everything, including your life, that's why! Think of those immoral things as a fire that could grow and spread and ultimately consume your child's life. If you do, you will start to monitor what you watch as well as what they watch.

Let me ask you a question: If you have televisions in your house, do you also have Christian television networks and programming to watch? Many cable companies do not provide it because there is not a demand for it. Get satellite so that you can have access to many of them; it's about the same cost as cable. Add to your satellite package the "sky angel" (www.skyangel.com) service! If Christians will choose to watch and ask for Christian stations, those stations will become a premium item because us "born-againers" account for a large segment of the television audience. The problem is…we are simply watching what everyone else is watching. I find many times that Christians are more critical of Christian television and programming than they are of the secular programming. We talk about how there is "nothing on" or how "immoral" television is, but then we say, "Well, what are you gonna do?" and then we watch it anyway!

How about you? Do you make Christian radio, television, and programming available to your children in your home? The more of us who watch and listen, the better the program production can become as we get behind it. The TBN, Daystar, CBN, Golden Eagle Broadcasting, WHT, JCTV, Word, and Church Channel networks are seen throughout the world, among many other kingdom advancing networks. The programming will only get better as we give them our support.

I go out on a limb here and present to you something that I discern in the Spirit. As this revolution grows, and the Church begins to handle its money in biblical ways, at least one of the Christian networks will buy one of the three major networks before that great day of the calling away of the Church!

So what does this have to do with teaching biblical principles of finance to our children? It has a lot to do with it. I have said before that when it comes to finances, we have been taught by the world and not by the Word. What do you think the most effective method of teaching the world's ways is? The media for sure! In general, the liberal media, not the Word, has influenced our ethical and political views; we have become accustomed to a certain level of violence and sexuality, and as time goes on, that level has increased. A number of years ago, the movie rating industry relaxed the rules and added PG-13. Many PG rated and PG-13 movies would have been rated R in the '70s. For example, the movie "The Graduate" was rated R in the late 1960s, yet today it is rated PG...suitable for kids? Why did they do this? There were too many R-rated movies and it was hurting ticket sales. We Americans just went along with it. The Parents' Television Counsel (www.parentstv.org) has done a great job at keeping us informed and effecting change in this area. If you have not joined their effort and you are concerned about these issues, you should contact them and add your support.

The media teaches our children that buying on credit is the American way and the "Why wait when you can have it now" way of thinking. I remember toy ads enticing me to be the first kid on the block to own a particular item and encouraging me to beg my parents to get it for me. This all happened when they were out of the room because they did not watch those kid shows. Remember the toy "Cool Shopping Barbie" that we talked about in Chapter 8? Our children's financial understanding is shaped by what they are seeing on television, not by the Word of God.

I grew up going to a great Christian school, went to a well-known Christian college, and attended great churches over the years; but nowhere did anyone teach me biblical principles of finance. In spite of all the financial difficulties of the baby boomer generation, we, too, for the most part, have not taught our children financial principles.

Why should we teach our children biblical principles of finance? Consider the following reasons:

1. *To prepare them for a time of testing in the area of finances.* We all want our children to succeed, to have faith in God, to have good marriages, and to be happy. Remember that nothing competes more for our affection for Christ than financial issues, and that over half of all divorces are rooted in financial difficulties. That is reason enough. We all know that no matter who we are, a time of testing will come in our lives. Our children need to have a strong faith in Christ and in the financial principles of the Word in order to survive these storms that most definitely will come their way. Whatever we can say about Jacob, one thing for sure is that he taught his son, Joseph, to honor God and not compromise no matter what the circumstances. And when Joseph's time of testing came, he stood the test and received the rewards of obedience. Psalm 105:17-24 summarizes Joseph's experiences in Egypt:

> *He sent a man before them, even Joseph, who was sold for a servant: whose feet they hurt with fetters: he was laid in iron: until the time that his word came: the word of the Lord tried him. The king sent and loosed him; even the ruler of the people, and let him go free. He made him lord of his house, and ruler of all his substance: to bind his princes at his pleasure; and teach his senators wisdom. Israel also came into Egypt; and Jacob sojourned in the land of Ham. And he*

increased his people greatly; and made them stronger than their enemies. (KJV)

It is interesting to note that the time of testing for Joseph and also for Daniel, as well as for many great men of God throughout history, came when they were about the age of 17. Even my son Ben, who has a deep commitment to serve the Lord, faced a test at the age of 17 when a doctor's diagnosis seemed to stand in the way of him pursuing a career in Christian television production. At the time of the diagnosis, while well-meaning Christians and doctors tried to talk him out of faith in God's healing power, Ben said, "I am not going to let my circumstances change my faith; I am going to let my faith change my circumstances." While we wait the manifestation of God's full healing, Ben is pursuing his calling, traveling 1,200 miles away from home to attend the God-honoring university of his choice, and is actively working in the production of Christian television while doing so. Watch for the testimony—it's coming! This paragraph in this book stands as a marker of Ben's faith and his family's faith.

I firmly believe that we must provide a Christ-centered education for our children. I graduated from the Delaware County Christian School in the Philadelphia area and Houghton College in New York (where I found my wife, Andrea). I credit my teachers and professors for much of the groundwork that eventually led to my ministry. When possible, I believe that believers should enroll their children in a "quality" (some unfortunately are without excellence) Christian school or home school or a combination of the two. When my children, Mindy and Ben, graduated from high school, they considered only excellent colleges where God is honored. Their choices were in line with the wishes that Andrea and I had for them and the principles we taught them. We never had to impose them upon Mindy and Ben because by age 18, they both had incorporated biblical values as most important to their education. Ben chose a Christian university 1,200 miles away despite his circumstances, even though two secular universities well-known in the mass media communication studies are within one hour of our home. Christian colleges and universities have become some of the world's most excellent institutions of higher learning. I firmly believe, especially in light of some of the liberal, Christian-mocking, non-biblical teaching and professors at many of our secular universities, that first and foremost, Christian children should seek to attend a college where God is honored. It has become a major problem in many Christian homes when a child who is not firmly grounded in the Word attends one of these institutions. They are easily led from the truth of the Word by professors and other students who do not honor God. Persecution of Christian students at secular universities is growing as well and the pressure is great.

We need to prepare our children! What if they not only develop a love for God but also for His Word? They would be prepared for any test!

2. *To cause them to seek direction in the area of finances.* Because they have a love for God and for His Word, they will seek out direction in making financial decisions as well as in other areas of their life. Too many financial decisions today are made by God's people using only worldly wisdom when the Word of God should be our guide for every financial or other decision of our life.

3. *To cause them to know the Word well enough to live it.* What if they knew the Word well enough to walk it, talk it, and most importantly, do it? That's what the Word calls "walking in the light" (see 1 Jn. 1:7). Then they would not be led astray by the false teachings of the world that do not line up with the Word of God. I have said before how amazed I am by how many Christians, who have been Christians for many years, espouse views that are contrary to Scripture simply because they do not know what the Word says on a particular issue or they have never taken the time to learn the Word. Attending classes in a medical school does not make you a competent physician. You must also study medical texts and put the information in your head for immediate recall. You must pass tests and practice what you are learning in order to be effective. It is the same for the believer. You can't just attend classes on Sunday and expect to pass the tests of life and think you have enough information to understand what God's purpose and calling is for your life. We cannot only be what I call "pew polishers" and then *infect* and *affect* the world for Christ!

I recall a man who told me how he had come to know the Lord. For many years he had desired to know more of God but knew no one who could answer his questions. Therefore, he began to seek God on his own and read the Bible, and then one day decided to attend a church in his neighborhood. There at this church one Sunday, he heard the answers to all his questions—how he could be sure that he would go to Heaven and why Jesus had to die in order for that to happen. He received Christ as Lord of his life that Sunday morning and subsequently made an appointment with the pastor so that he could ask more questions that were on his mind. On his way out of church that morning, he saw a man in the crowd with whom he had worked and ate lunch with for many years. Excited to see a face he knew, he went to him and exclaimed, "I did not know you were going to church. I just started coming this week. How long have you been coming here?" The man replied, "Oh, almost all my life. I'm a deacon here!" The new believer then proceeded to ask him why he had never told him about Jesus.

I think the message here is loud and clear. Someone once asked, "If you were on trial for being a Christian, would there be enough evidence to convict you?"

4. *To cause them to grow up learning to be obedient to the Lord in their finances.* How I wish there would have been financial programs like there are today, available to my wife and me when we were growing up. Perhaps much of the heartache and the difficult times would not have happened. But even though there are educational resources available to teach children financial principles, things have not changed much. Few churches or Christian schools make teaching biblical financial principles to children a regular part of their Christian education curriculum. There are programs, including Crown Financial Ministry programs for small children, pre-teens, teenagers, and college-age groups; but as I said, few churches or Christian schools have incorporated them into their curriculum.

We can learn something from the terrorist group Hamas in Israel who knows very well that if you want to create long-lasting change, you must teach children when they are young and impressionable. They teach their children almost from the time they are born to hate the Jews, and that fighting and dying for their cause is honorable and just. Consequently, their younger generation is extremely ruthless in the pursuit of their evil cause. Imagine if the Church, and parents in specific, took the time to teach their children the Word so that as they grow up, they internalize it and incorporate it into their adult lives. What a difference it would make in the effectiveness of the ministry of the Church in general! But how can we teach it if we ourselves don't know it?

We have got to address this issue, and again the Barna organization gives us some additional insight into what is going on. In September 2003, their website (http:/barna.org) reported the results of a study of the "twenty somethings" (those 20 to 30 years old). The results revealed that less than 30 percent attended church in a typical week and less than 30 percent gave any type of a donation to a ministry in the previous year. You may say, "Well, the church has really fallen down in this area," and that may be true. I want to remind you, however, that the main responsibility to teach children rests upon their parents.

Do you know what the main reason is that parents don't teach their children the Word and specifically teach them what it says about handling money and possessions?

They don't know the Word themselves!

This must become a family project in many areas. Perhaps we could use some of the time we spend watching our favorite program or movie learning something that has eternal significance.

Are you willing to make the sacrifice?

I have always said, *sacrifice the time or sacrifice the children!* Which sacrifice are you going to make? It is better to build children than to be faced with fixing or correcting adults.

What if our children grew up knowing...

So if you have not been trustworthy in handling worldly wealth, who will trust you with true riches? (Luke 16:11).

What if they knew...

Everything in the heavens and earth is Yours, Oh Lord, and this is Your Kingdom. We adore You as being in control of everything. Riches and honor come from You, oh Lord, and You are the ruler of all mankind: Your hand controls power and might and it is at Your discretion that men are made great and given strength (1 Chronicles 29:11-12 LB).

What if they knew…

Moreover it is required in stewards, that a man be found faithful (1 Corinthians 4:2 KJV).

The rich rule over the poor, and the borrower is servant to the lender (Proverbs 22:7).

What if they knew…

1. The second most talked about subject in the Bible is handling money and possessions.

2. There are 2,350 verses in the Bible regarding handling every aspect of money.

3. There are 126 biblical financial principles taught in the New Testament alone.

4. Over one half of the parables Jesus taught were about handling money and possessions.

We need to teach our children what many of us need to know as well. The tests and trials of life are coming. Our children's success (and our success as well) in walking out those tests depends solely on the relationship they have personally (not their parent's relationship) built with the Lord Jesus and of their understanding and implementation of God's Word in their lives.

Would you send your child out into the bitter cold weather without a coat, hat, and gloves? No, you would not! Too often, however, we let them grow up and go out into the world totally unprepared for what they are about to face.

Remember the illustration I gave of the playground without the fence in Chapter 8—how the children playing would occasionally run into the road and be hit by a car. It was not hard for the church to vote to put a fence up, was it? However, every day, our children are growing up and running out into the street of financial difficulties and disaster…yet we haven't put the fence up! It is time we get hold of the educational resources available to us today and put up that fence!

The lives of our children depend on it!

CHAPTER *13*

INVESTING

An investment is anything that you put money into, in which you expect a return *of* your money and a return *on* your money. Investing is saving your money and growing that money while it is saved. Proverbs 21:20 says, "The wise man saves for the future, but the foolish man spends whatever he gets!" (LB). What is the best way to save money? "Steady plodding brings prosperity" (Prov. 21:5 LB). Paraphrase that verse—little by little saved on a regular basis develops financial security!

The poverty theologian would say that the Christian should not invest but should depend on God, using the story of the rich young ruler in Luke chapter 18 as support and evidence. The rich young ruler was told by Jesus to go sell all he had and to give it to the poor. However, Jesus was dealing with a heart commitment here, not a poverty commitment, because He knew that the young ruler's heart was not right. This example shows human greed and the lure of worldly wealth, not the need to be poor in order to be acceptable to Jesus. Although I agree with the poverty theologian that the Christian should depend on God, the rest of his thinking is not biblical. We have already reviewed Scripture to refute that narrow view.

Some years ago, I worked with a client who attended a church where the pastor reviewed the congregation's finances with them and encouraged them to give their savings and life insurance cash values to the church. It was a fast-growing church and the "talk of the town." They bought a big house for cash and converted it into a church. My client eventually ceased being my client because all insurance and investments had been liquidated.

A few years later, I became aware of the fact that there were problems at the church and that the pastor was being challenged on certain practices by some of the individuals in the church as well as some of the other pastors in town who were counseling with the individuals who had been hurt by his actions. Soon after, the pastor resigned and moved out of the area. Today, he is not in the pastorate. The church building is now a law office, and the members have been absorbed into other evangelical churches in town.

After one of my speaking engagements, a man who looked somewhat familiar, approached me. I soon recognized him as this previous client who I had not seen in years. He reminded me that he had cashed in his funds, and on the pastor's recommendation invested in gold and silver. He lost all his money when he could not meet a margin call. (Remember this subject from Chapter 8 regarding credit...margin is not biblical!) One of his children had died suddenly and because there was no longer any family life insurance, the grieving family was also set back financially. Here he was ten years later, starting to rebuild all over again. Unfortunately, this is not a unique situation. I have seen it often in my experience over the years.

Folks, this is not God's way. This is not how pastors are to lead their flock. We are to invest as the Master instructed! Pastors, we will address your role in the finances of your people in a subsequent chapter, but please don't get swallowed up by this gold-and-silver routine that seems to recycle itself in Christian circles every so often.

Tell me, if we are moving to a cashless society as the Bible indicates we will in the last days, what good will your gold and silver be? Besides, they have proven over and over in my experience in this business to be inconsistent and unreliable investments.

I have seen all too often pastors using the pulpit to give investment advice. This is not wisdom and has usually caused grief in the long run for the pastor. I have been appalled at some of the advice I have heard from the pulpit, on the radio, and on television. Remember, the right thing for one individual may not be the right thing for another. This is the reason why the NASD (National Association of Securities Dealers) does not allow licensed financial advisors to give general advice in this way. The rules are strict!

I will never forget the advice of Rev. Claude Ries, former professor at Houghton College and longtime pastor. Dr. Ries, known as the "pastor's pastor" at the time, was in his 80's and retired. He came and addressed the ministerial students, and among other things offered this advice. He looked at us all and implored us to listen and pay special heed to these words: "Gentlemen, never, never, never use the pulpit as a political soapbox or to give financial advice—never, never. Just preach the Word! You will never know the numbers I have counseled, the heartache, the grief of those who have not followed this advice." You see, the Bible provides the guidelines to make the right decisions in political and financial issues, and we are to teach our people those principles.

I have also helped people who listened to bad advice from the pulpit—advice that was not biblical or correct, but based on clichés. We must teach the financial principles in the Word, not put our own spin on the latest financial news from Wall Street's "talking heads." They operate under a different system and a different set of values—systems and values unfortunately found too often in the church.

Biblically speaking then, as a Christian, what should our investment goals be? I believe there are four goals according to Scripture with numerous passages to support each. Let me summarize them here:

1. To provide for and to protect our family.

2. To develop working capital and emergency funds.

3. To be able to see a need within the Kingdom and fill it through giving.

4. To become financially independent and free to serve the Lord.

Hmmm. Did you notice what is missing? How about retirement? Did you know that retirement is not taught anywhere in the Bible? I believe that #4 replaces retirement. The Christian has been charged with a mission all his life. That mission is to go into the entire world and preach the gospel. The Christian should strive to be financially independent to assist in full-time ministry. Imagine if Christians were such good stewards that they could retire early from their careers and devote their time to Kingdom work without needing to accept any type of payment! What an impact! I know people like that. Their investment income supports their ministry efforts by supporting them. What about you? What do you plan to do with your retirement? How about working in a ministry and providing your talents to advance the Kingdom while living off investment income? We in the Church have sent far too many "missionaries" to the golf courses and retirement communities of this country while there is still harvest in the fields. Put yourself and your, excuse me, *His* money to work. Don't hoard it!

Yes, I help Christians plan for "retirement," but I encourage them to consider planning for full-time Christian service. My friend Howard Dayton, CEO of Crown Financial Ministries, refers to this as "being financially free to serve Him."

The Bible not only tells us to invest and to save, but it also teaches the successful investment strategies we use in the investment world all the time. Wall Street thinks they were the first to think of these, but...nope...they're in the Bible! Following are a few strategies with a brief commentary on each:

1. Risk Evaluation: "There is another serious problem I have seen everywhere; savings are put into risky investments that turn sour, and soon there is nothing left to pass on to one's son. The man who speculates is soon back to where he began—with nothing" (Eccl. 5:13-15 LB). Here is another one: "A prudent man sees danger and protects himself" (Prov. 22:3 LB).

2. Invest for Ownership: The Israelites were taught to take an ownership position in the land (see Deut. 19:2,14). The parable of the ten minas teaches that you should put the money to work, not hoard it (see Luke 19).

3. Dollar Cost Averaging: "Steady plodding brings prosperity" (Prov. 21:5 LB). Basically, the strategy and the verse both say that a little bit invested regularly over a long period of time becomes a lot!

4. Asset Allocation or Portfolio Balancing: "Give portions to seven, yes to eight, for you do not know what disaster may come upon the land" (Eccl. 11:2).

5. Market Timing and Sector Rotation: "There is a time for everything, and a season for every activity under heaven" (Eccl. 3:1).

The verses above contain just a sampling of investment strategies taught in the great Financial Manual, the Bible! Now let's take a look at a few investments that compete for the money entrusted us by the Master.

Types of Investments

General categories of investments that are available today include:

1. *Guarantees:* This type includes such things as fixed annuities, CD's, (certificates of deposit), whole life insurance, and universal life insurance.

2. *Equities:* These include such things as mutual funds, stocks, bonds, variable annuities, and variable life insurance.

3. *Speculative:* These include such things as commodities, tax shelters, coins, gems, silver, and gold.

4. *Real:* This refers to real property or real estate.

After reviewing these types of investments, I have come up with a guideline list of the best and worst. I've also discovered while reading Larry Burkett's book, *Investing for the Future,* that his list is in agreement with mine. Use this as a guideline in the development of your investment program.

Worst Investments for the Steward

1. Precious Metals and Gemstones.

2. Collectibles.

3. Coins.

4. Commodities.

5. Limited partnerships (tax shelters).

6. Gold and silver.

7. Stocks purchased individually (I know you're surprised—read on).

You may be in agreement with some of these items, and you may be surprised at others. I am not saying that you cannot make money in these areas; you may know someone who has. But the risk and volatility are great; there are just too many variables. During my many years of experience in the financial industry, I have known few to ever make money in numbers 1, 2, 3, 4, 5, and 6. Oh yes, they may have made money on a short-term basis, but usually the results came crashing down. Tax shelters in limited partnerships have frequently been good for saving taxes because if you don't make anything or if you lose the money, that still does not hurt you tax-wise! Some of you professionals who have invested in these to reduce your taxes know what I mean!

What about #7—stocks? Here, I am talking about investing in individual stocks. Why is this risky and too often unprofitable? First, you cannot get as diversified a portfolio in individual stocks as you can in stock mutual funds for the amount of money the average person has to invest. Secondly, many people are not skilled in selecting stocks and only do so by name recognition, or a gut feeling, or because someone else did. These are not smart ways to choose stocks.

What about going to a stockbroker? Now this is important—listen to what I have to say! He or she is in the business of selling you stocks. They do not make money unless they create a transaction. If he or she works for an investment firm which also underwrites issues of new stock—and the big ones do—guess what? You are the one they push their inventory off on! The Wall Street Journal in June 1999 reported the results of the stock picks of major wire houses, and most did not fare well—*and that was during a bull market!* CBS News in February 2001 reported that analysts are pressured to make certain stocks look good; after all, they said, it is estimated that brokerage houses make 70 percent of their profits from what is called investment banking, which is raising money for companies that need cash. Major brokerage houses are actually cheerleaders for certain stocks of client companies or companies they would like as clients. If you are a broker reading these words, I know how you feel because I know how I felt when I discovered these things. I first rejected them until the Lord showed me His more excellent way, and it was costly for me to make the switch. I say leave the stock picking to the pros—money managers who do not have an interest in moving certain stocks, but choose stocks based on performance, potential, and portfolio fit! Develop a financial plan and then pick investments to fit the overall plan. In the next chapter on financial planning, we will discuss this further.

The late Edwin Kennedy, former director and CEO of Lehman Brothers made a lot of money in individual stocks, and he should have—he was a pro! He was a wonderful man and a dear friend of mine and of my family. We affectionately called him "O'pah." I loved sitting at his feet and picking his mind on financial issues. I was so blessed to have him as a friend and as a resource.

One day, he and I were sitting in his living room at his lake house, chatting about investments (what else?), and I asked him a question. "O'pah, if you were a man of 25 today and just starting out in your financial planning, how would you invest?" I had not shared my view with him yet on individual stock investing. (This guy was a pro and my mama didn't raise no fool!)

I was surprised at his response. He acknowledged that individual stock investments had been good to him, but that he had always had good research available to him in making his decisions and he was a professional. He said, "You know, Buck, I have thought about that, and my answer would be mutual funds! Yes, I would find some good mutual funds with good management and a good track record, and I would start there."

Wow, O'pah was even smarter than I thought! He agreed with me!

I told him how I felt and that I was surprised he had the same view. He continued, "If you use mutual funds, it is so much easier to diversify and get that balance that I strove for in my portfolio all my investing life. Over the long term, that produces better results than buying and selling individual stocks."

I include stocks on this list based on my own experience as well. I, along with my clients, have seen, on the average, better consistent growth in a portfolio of asset allocated mutual funds, than I have with individual stock investors of average assets. Oh yes, I have seen people who have made money in individual stocks, but clients using mutual funds over the long term have fared much better. Mutual funds are easier to work with in retirement as well. It is usually easier to set up regular monthly income from investments.

BEST INVESTMENTS FOR THE STEWARD

1. *Real Estate.* Your home and income properties (only if you know how to buy income properties and manage them. If you don't, it's a good way to lose your shirt!)

2. *Mutual Funds* (pooling your money with other investors and having professionals choose the stocks and bonds in which to invest).

3. *Insurance Company Products.*

   Annuities (when used properly, but possibly the most abused in their use).

   Life Insurance (for family security, not really for investment purposes).

   Whole Life (guarantees provided by this kind).

   Universal and Variable (these are more investment oriented.)

   (Note: Term is not an investment, just pure insurance.)

4. *Company Retirement Plans; IRA Accounts.*

5. *Government Backed Securities.*

Regarding life insurance, I could have written a whole chapter on this topic, but for our purposes now, we will make just a few brief comments. Life insurance is the backbone of your financial plan. As with investments, there is no "one size fits all" plan for everyone, even though you will hear generalized clichés about what life insurance can do for you. The different types of life insurance are designed for different needs and applications. An insurance program should be tailored to fit your financial plan (more on that in the next chapter). After nearly 30 years in this business, I have grown tired of hearing the general advice, "Buy term and invest the difference." This cliché has been thrown around so much that people believe it applies to everyone, when in fact, it is shortsighted and is more of a half-truth. Let me explain.

This philosophy originally was promoted by the brokerage houses and some mutual fund sales organizations that recognized the enormous amount of money sitting in cash value or what is known as whole life insurance. They had a hidden agenda—they recognized a huge market for their stocks and mutual funds if they could just get people to tap into these contracts and give them the cash value in trade for equities (stocks, mutual funds). The first step was to get the brokers licensed to sell insurance and give them a good term life insurance product to trade for the cash value life insurance of the clients. The brokerages then proceeded to discredit cash value life insurance as a poor "investment." (It was never designed to be an investment; it is insurance.) Subsequently, many people cashed in their life insurance on their advice to buy equities.

Many just cashed in, bought term, and *spent* the difference.

The fact of the matter is that you must look at the whole picture when it comes to life insurance. So what's the problem?

I have been involved in a lot of estate planning, and I have found, as other estate planners today will also tell you, that many of the same people, who 20 to 25 years ago cashed in their life insurance to buy stocks, are now purchasing cash value, permanent life insurance today at higher rates due to their age. They are purchasing it to protect their assets from erosion due to estate or income taxes on "qualified" (IRA, 401K or other types of retirement) accounts. In fact, the industry developed what is known as "second to die" or "joint and survivor" life insurance products for the purpose of aiding older people with this type of problem. I have heard more than once some unkind words for the guy who years before talked them into cashing in their life insurance years before to buy stocks or mutual funds.

The life insurance industry estimates that for 96 percent of all term policies ever written, a death claim has never been paid. The reason is, the policies are not in force at the time the person dies! The plan either became too expensive to continue as the person got older, or in some cases, it could not be renewed. These estate planning "term only buyers" then eventually discovered that the only option was to buy cash value, permanent life insurance at the most expensive time of their lives.

Remember, I said that the cliché, "Buy term and invest the difference" was a half-truth. It is a half-truth because it is partly right. An average person throughout his life will need more life insurance when he is raising a family than during his retirement. The best way to meet a temporary larger need is with term life insurance and to invest for short-term and educational needs. However, as we move into the empty nest phase of our life, we need to carry some permanent life insurance into retirement. The proper amount of permanent life insurance will allow a retiree to take maximum payouts on his or her pension because a surviving spouse's income is protected by the proceeds of the life insurance. This is known as a "pension maximization program."

Another reason permanent life insurance is needed is because today there are many people carrying 401Ks, IRAs, and other retirement programs with large balances into retirement; consequently, their life insurance can be used by their heirs to pay the taxes due when they pass this money on to their heirs and hopefully into Kingdom work as well. Life insurance usage will change over the life of the insured from providing security for the family to protecting their estate from erosion due to taxes. One can also become quite creative with life insurance when setting up planned gifts to ministries—another excellent reason to consider permanent life insurance. Term insurance can only do the first half! Then it expires, gets too expensive, and is gone! In fact, a little known fact is that if term insurance is kept for a long term, it usually becomes more expensive when compared side by side with a universal, variable, or even whole life insurance plan.

The point is, when it comes to insurance, investments, and general financial planning principles, beware of the "one size fits all" clichés. We all are different! That is why we all don't wear the same size clothing or the same style clothes or drive the same kind of car. Because our circumstances are different, our planning must be "sized to fit."

In any investments, it is wise to seek godly counsel from someone who knows biblical principles, has a record of accomplishment, and has developed a committed and submitted relationship with the Lord. Many so-called advisors are merely brokers looking for securities transactions or insurance agents looking for insurance sales. Some have a few letters after their name because they have completed a course, but that doesn't mean they have experience or expertise. Many of these lettered people are not licensed by a government agency to assist you in implementing the program. An accountant is a tax and accounting advisor; he is not a financial advisor. Likewise, an attorney is a legal advisor, not a financial advisor. I work with individuals in both professions as my clients, and I personally have an attorney and an accountant. They represent different fields; do not get all your financial advice from them. Remember, there are financial advisors who are Christians, and there are Christian financial advisors—these are two different things. The first is a Christian who gives worldly advice the institutions have taught him to give; the second gives advice based on biblical principles. How do you know which is which? Learn biblical principles regarding finance for yourself, and the Word will guide you. We will discuss choosing an advisor further in the next chapter.

My point is: Do not be afraid to seek advice; it is wise and biblical to do so.

Another area of concern to Christians is where their money is invested. The wealth of many Christians, and what is even worse, the funds of ministries, are invested in mutual funds or stocks of companies that are involved in things contrary to biblical values. The promotion of abortion, pornography, alcohol, tobacco, and anti-family lifestyles is commonly found in many companies whose stocks are often held by Christians or ministry organizations. Many advisors including Christian ones say there is no way to protect yourself from this situation. They are either uninformed or cannot provide you with the screened investments!

On the other hand, many broker-dealers will not contract with these morally responsible funds because the funds are considered "politically incorrect." The broker-dealer companies are concerned about a backlash from special interest groups. Today there is not only screening software available so that you can study various funds to determine the level of biblical violations within them, there is also Christian value-based mutual funds. These funds hire top-ranked money managers and provide them with a list of companies they are not allowed to hold in the portfolio. The Timothy Plan is a pioneer in morally based mutual funds and has been successful in using its influence as a major stockholder to influence the policies of the companies it invests in.

Imagine what influence we could exert in this world if Christians invested with their values in mind and we did it together!

Today, even choosing a bank that follows biblical principles is becoming an option to the believer. Contact my ministry offices for more information regarding both of these opportunities.

Beware of get-rich schemes, "hot tips," "sure things," and "unique opportunities." I so tire of hearing of these things, especially in light of the fact that the Bible says, "Steady plodding brings prosperity, hasty speculation brings poverty" (Prov. 21:5 LB). I am not talking as one who is above it all; I have learned most of the stuff that is in this book the hard way. I understand!

You have heard it said, "If it sounds too good to be true, it probably is!" Not only are you as an individual susceptible to these schemes, but ministries are as well. Even well-known ministries have made mistakes because they never learned what the Bible teaches in the area of finances.

I remember in the early '90s, I received a call and a 13-page fax of information from a representative of a national ministry. He asked me my opinion on an opportunity that the ministry was presented with to "invest" their foundation funds in such a manner as to double the money through the use of anonymous investors. This possibly well-meaning organization promised this ministry that it would increase their revenue substantially, enabling the ministry to accomplish more.

I reviewed the material and called him back. I told him what the Scriptures say concerning get-rich-quick schemes, and that this opportunity appeared to me to be somewhat of a "Ponzi scheme." The firm presenting the offer had not provided real information of what would happen to the money when it was turned over, other than it would be doubled and returned. It could then be invested again if they wished. But what happened to the money and how it was invested was all too much of a secret. I told him that if I were him, I would decline to take the opportunity if for no other reason than the biblical one, and that was reason enough! I remember saying that if the presenting organization could fulfill their promise, then why had not Wall Street already done it or other investment firms set themselves up as custodians.

This ministry took my advice, and I never heard of it again until one day when I was watching the news.

Does anyone out there remember a firm called New Era? When the news broke, I learned that many ministries had become involved (most without seeking professional godly advice). At the beginning, as some doubled their money as was promised, more got involved. But eventually, ministries that were close to my heart fell into danger of losing it all, in what the authorities called a "Ponzi scheme." I was sick. It was just what I thought it would be, and I wished I had taken a more proactive role with other ministries.

How did it happen? Simply put, the leadership of the ministries had not known what the Bible says about money and that it warns specifically against such investments. Many did not seek godly counsel from qualified *godly* investment people having an understanding of biblical principles. They did not get enough information—no "due diligence," as my attorney friends would say. Many invested on the theory, "Well, Joe made money, so I'm gonna get in!" Since then, I have heard of various "schemes" that have circulated within the Body of Christ. Even at the time of this writing, I am investigating some things that have been reported to me.

A general caution: Beware of those investment offers that promise larger returns than you can make through traditional investments, and offer incentives for you to find others to join in. These opportunities often will not provide you the name of the money managers or give you a good explanation of how these funds are being invested. Success is not always a good indicator, because even a Ponzi scheme works for a season until the demands on it become greater than the supply. You see, for an investment to work, it has to have a supply from a source outside of new investors, a source to whom no obligation for repayment is required. This is called a "return on investment." In a Ponzi scheme, you are simply being repaid and given your "return" from the funds of new investors. These types of schemes often work well on paper, often misleading professionals who do not know what the Bible says on this subject. Even many godly, well-meaning people are led astray in an effort to "raise money quickly for the Kingdom."

Listen, this is so important! God doesn't need schemes to generate money quickly. Remember Psalm 24:1: "The earth is the Lord's!" He already has it! In order to move it in your direction or toward the needs of the Kingdom, all He needs is your obedience! Remember, in the Kingdom, prosperity and obedience mean the same thing. Note that Jesus took a little boy's two-piece fish dinner with biscuits and fed the whole crowd with it, and still had some left over to send to the food pantry! (See John chapter 6.) He did not start a food scheme and get others to join in!

First Timothy 6:9-10 says, "People who want to get rich fall into temptation and a trap and into many foolish and harmful desires that plunge men into ruin and destruction. For the love of money is a root of all kinds of evil. Some people, eager for money, have wandered from the faith and pierced themselves with many grieves." I did not make this opinion up! The enemy will attempt to trap us. He has done it before; he will do it again unless we learn what the Word says. We can wander from the faith, from the faith in the Word, by not knowing God's will regarding money, which will cause us much grief. There were many embarrassed ministries, embarrassed leaders, and much grief. Why? Simply, they did not know the Scriptures. Investing in New Era was not a biblical investment; there was no ownership! It was a get-rich-quick scheme! The source of the return was never identified.

I wanted to start a revolution.

I pray I have!

Have I convinced you to sign on to it? The Kingdom is waiting!

Proverbs 27:12b tells us, "The naive proceed and pay the penalty" (RSV). Remember that investing takes discipline and wisdom, and you may not make a bundle over night! God gives us a better plan. Remember the "steady plodding" part and do it! The Christian's investment slogan, in my opinion, should be, "Steady plod till you're free to serve God!" I cannot tell you how often I have seen people become obedient and begin to "steady plod," and then receive what I call "suddenly blessings" from God because of their faithfulness. Decide right now to follow God's financial plan for you and watch your own story unfold.

My intent here is to give an overview of the problems and to call us to financial faithfulness. In order to get comprehensive advice on investing, godly counsel should be sought in the light of *your* own personal situation. There is no advice that applies to everyone, for all our circumstances are different. An investment strategy must be developed that is suitable to your individual circumstances.

Remember, there is no better investment than investing in souls!

Let's move on to talk about developing your own financial plan.

CHAPTER 14

FINANCIAL PLANNING

...Write the vision, and make it plain upon tables, that he may run that readeth it (Habakkuk 2:2 KJV).

You can be a saver or an investor, but yet not have a financial plan. In fact, you may have accumulated substantial assets but still not have a financial plan. A financial plan is a written vision for your financial future, stating what your specific goals are and how you plan to accomplish those goals. The plan is developed with the flexibility to change as your life circumstances change, and it requires constant monitoring and updating. Jesus said:

For which of you, intending to build a tower, sitteth not down first, and counteth the cost, whether he have sufficient to finish it? (Luke 14:28 KJV)

Over the years, many people have met with me and brought with them what I refer to as a "box of component parts." In the box, they might have information on their 401K or other IRA-type programs, life insurance, investments, and savings. But although they have accumulated assets, they have no plan or purpose as to how these things are going to harmoniously work together to help them arrive at their goals. In many instances, these people are not even sure what their goals are. In most cases, they have not even thought about it. They are doing these things just because they have heard that you are supposed to do them and know others are doing likewise.

Let me illustrate this another way. Suppose a friend invites me over to his house to see his new car, and when I arrive there, he takes me to his garage. When he raises the door and I peer in, I see nothing but boxes of parts, fenders, seats, tires, and such, piled in the garage. "Where's the car?" I ask. He replies that it is all there, that every part of a particular model car is there in the garage. "What kind of car is it?" I ask. He replies that he is not really sure because he does not understand how the car goes together or what it will look like.

I say to him, "In reality, you don't have a new car but a garage full of component parts. Are you even sure that all the parts of this particular car are there, or if they are even the right parts?" I further suggest to him that he should consider hiring a mechanic to assemble the car, to determine whether anything else is needed, and to organize the component parts in the proper way so he can see exactly what he has, how they all fit together, and then actually use the car to take him where he wants to go.

Now you may think this story is odd and that my friend is not very bright to have not recognized his problem before now. And I would have to agree. The fact is, however, that this is exactly what most people do with their finances. They collect component parts but have no vision of what it is and where it is going to take them; yet they conclude that they have a financial plan. In reality, they need help to pull all these things together, and they should seek *godly* (Bible-centered) counsel in this area.

I have never enjoyed the task of trying to help someone at retirement age, who has made his own investment decisions or left them up to a broker and who has never developed a financial plan, pull together their component parts and try to make them work. Sometimes we have had to do some radical things in order to help them receive the retirement income they need. However, if they had been following a financial plan earlier in life, they would have been methodically preparing in advance for this day and would have already had things in position to accomplish what we needed to do at that moment.

Let's talk briefly about what a financial plan is. I could write a whole book on this subject alone, but for our purposes, I will give you an overview of what a plan should include.

There are some basic tenets of a financial plan that must be considered and reprioritized over the years as you develop and fine-tune it. *A financial plan, just like me, is always a work in progress!* I tell my clients when they come to me, that I immediately picture them on a time line. I find out when they were born, and we determine the season of time when they will most likely go home to be with the Lord. I then place them on the time line based on their current age and review what they have accomplished financially. I then proceed, based on their goals, to project where they are going and what they need to do in order to achieve what they have set in their mind to do, before they literally "get to the end of the line." We also build in to the scenario an emergency system in the case of an earlier death than projected. We continue to talk about what happens at that point—specifically, their estate plans. This time line would look something like this:

/—/ —— / ———————— / —————— / ———— / ———— / — / — /

Birth   Education   Career & Beginning of Family   Children's Education   Empty Nest   Senior Years   Death   Eternity

Within that time line, different types of planning should occur and, of course, debt planning must be an important part of it because debt often prevents many of us from doing any type of planning to begin with. Basically, today, I find that the credit card companies and creditors are always anxious to take your retirement, ready assets, and children's education savings in the form of interest. This is why it is so important to save to develop ready assets right from the beginning so that you do not have to use credit to meet unexpected expenses. Children need to be taught to save so that at the beginning of their life they immediately have a cushion on which to build and these ready assets can function as a safety net.

I have found that the development of ready assets (money that is immediately available and liquid and not in any educational or retirement program) is usually the weakest area in the average financial plan This money also is often the source of our giving funds; consequently, the devil really does not want you to develop ready assets...it makes him sweat! (Speaking of giving funds, I even have clients who have developed an account expressly for the purpose of meeting emergency needs of ministries!)

The financial plan should first identify personal data of anyone who is covered by the plan, your short-term and long-term goals and objectives as well as identifying any issues and problems. A schedule listing assets and liabilities (a balance sheet) and a calculation of net worth are also included. Don't be embarrassed at this point and quit—that's exactly what the enemy will tell you to do. But if you don't follow the plan, things will never change financially, even if you are blessed with a large amount of money at some point in your life. Why? Eventually, the money will be spent because you had never developed the system or expertise to manage your money. Consequently, when you receive a windfall or blessing, it will be deposited into your "mismanagement system."

Do you have a management system or a mismanagement system?

A financial plan will help you develop a system of money management, with the most important tool in that system being the *budget* (there's that word again).

I mentioned that in the development of each individual financial plan, basic areas of concern are noted. These areas are then ranked in their order of priority based on the set goals and current situation. The ranking of these priorities will change as you move along the time line. Obviously, income from investments will be more important and of concern to a person who is retired than to a 30 year old who is still working and saving towards that day. They are not drawing income from what they are saving; they are growing it. Eventually, as the 30 year old moves along the time line, income from investments will become higher and higher in priority.

Following are a list of priority areas with a brief description of each:

1. *Family Security:* This area is usually most important for a young family with children still living at home, although it remains important throughout your whole life. Planning must be made for such things as a critical illness (health, disability, and long-term care insurance), death (life insurance), and catastrophic property losses (home, auto, and personal liability insurance, including business insurance, if appropriate). Insurance is the backbone of the financial plan.

2. *Liquidity:* How much financial liquidity you have determines how important this is at the current time. If you have none, then it is very important. You need an emergency contingency, giving fund like the one we discussed in Chapter 9 on money management. This is what keeps us from taking on more debt when an emergency arises; we are able to meet our own emergency needs. (I said "needs," not "wants"...most debt is accumulated in the pursuit of wants!)

3. *Safety:* An evaluation of the investments currently held and those planned for the future must be conducted. This evaluation considers such things as your risk tolerance and management, diversification of assets, liquidity, and suitability. I have found in my experience that many people have investments, but these investments are not suitable to their situation. Not long before writing this chapter, I met with a retired couple whose broker had never moved them out of the aggressive growth, higher-risk investments that they held when they were younger and which were appropriate for that time. The 9/11 downturn in the market had hurt them badly at a time when they needed to be in safer (less volatile) investments.

A week later, a 28-year-old man came to talk to me about his investments. He had experienced 80 to 90 percent losses and wanted my help. He had invested everything in high-risk stocks and had made a lot of money in a short time. He thought he was doing great and then it all came crashing down. Why? He had not diversified his investments and had not been maintaining a balanced portfolio. (His broker did okay through it all, except for the fact that he lost a client. The type of advice he gave usually costs a person his job in the advisory business—and that is good!) There was nothing I could do but counsel the young man and help him restructure and start over the right way.

4. *Long and Short-term Growth:* Investments must be evaluated as to whether they are positioned for short or long-term growth. Education and retirement can both be short or long-term investments depending on the age of the individual who will receive the benefits of the funds. Retirement funds, for example, should start out as long term, but as one approaches retirement and moves along the time line, the investments should be repositioned for short-term growth, and then positioned for capital preservation and income needs in retirement.

5. *Tax Advantage:* An evaluation of the tax situation is important in order to determine if adjustments need to be made to save tax dollars. One should not pay more taxes than he needs to, but he also needs to be reasonable in finding and using strategies to save tax dollars.

Today there is so much effort in the financial world to develop programs that help you to skirt tax laws. Highly compensated individuals who have already maximized their retirement programs want to do all they can to hold on to more money using other types of financial products. Many financial advisors latch onto these kinds of programs and seek potential clients because it is a lucrative business. In my earlier years, I was one of these types of advisors because that is what I was taught and encouraged to do. I really don't have any time for that type of business now because I believe that as a Christian we should not be looking for more programs that help us set aside money on a deferred basis or play games with tax law loopholes. This is called hoarding, and it is not biblical!

If you are a Christian and find that you have done everything within reason to save tax dollars and to prepare for education and retirement needs, and you are still paying substantial taxes…

I have a message for you.

You are being blessed by God! There is some reason God is giving you more of His money to manage. The question is: Are you passing or failing the "abundant blessing test"?

The answer?

Just give more to ministries advancing the Kingdom of Jesus Christ, and you will reduce your tax liability! Meanwhile, you're being obedient to the call of Christ in Luke 12:21 to be "rich toward God." If you are in this position, you have become what I call a "giving machine," which is what I dream of being!

As you give, you'll save tax dollars and in doing so, God will bless you in return so you can give again. And the cycle continues! Now that's fun!

I know people who are experiencing this type of life. The "blessing cycle" kicks in and God continues blessing them in their giving, and their ability to give keeps growing. But instead of deferring excess money for retirement that their executor ends up giving to the government when they die, they are laying up treasures in Heaven! They are sending what they would have paid to the tax man on ahead for their eternal use, converting it to crowns! They are investing in something that gives a guaranteed eternal return…they are investing in souls!

I know Christians who stop saving for retirement in their 50's because projections reveal that they have ample money to live on, and instead they give the money they had been giving to their retirement programs to advance the gospel of Jesus Christ. They have kicked into the mode of funding the great commission!

How about you? Are you running around seeking tax shelters and legal loopholes to save taxes? If you are, you are in danger of failing the "abundant blessing test." Wouldn't you rather be a giving machine?

Hmm…talk amongst yourselves!

6. *Income from Investments:* For those of you who are retirement age, widowed with children, a full-time student, or disabled, this becomes a major area of priority. Investments need to be structured based on living needs in order to provide the best possible income. This must be evaluated to determine if the best possible results are being realized.

As I previously stated, I am amazed at how many people bring me their statements when we begin the planning process and aren't aware of what they have or what their investments are to accomplish. They often have great difficulty even reading their statements. Now, I am the first to admit, as a professional, that many statements are confusing, especially from some of the brokerage houses that use a brokerage platform statement. It usually takes some studying if you can keep the pages organized and not get them mixed up or out of order. Sometimes it is time-consuming and difficult even with professional help.

Does anyone know what I am talking about out there? I hear some of you chuckling.

I have heard advisors from these firms say they prefer it that way because it makes it more difficult for clients to move their money elsewhere. Basically, what they are saying is, "Keep the client confused, and they won't leave you." I have even attended meetings and heard financial companies encourage advisors to set things up in this way to discourage a client from switching advisors!

The term *brokerage platform* refers to a situation where the advisory company sets up all accounts with different money managers on one statement—this statement lists the advisory company's name and local address. It may have mutual funds with other firms listed, but you do not receive a separate statement from each mutual fund company. Usually, they like to use their own "proprietary" investments. The platform is used instead of setting up the account directly with the investment company. Typically, once the account is set up directly with the money managers, transfers and exchanges within that fund family are free of any charges imposed by the advisory firm.

Do not misunderstand me; I am not against the use of the brokerage platform, and I admit that it is simpler (if you can read and understand it) to have all your accounts listed on one page, but it also makes it easier to hide abuses. There are often charges for moving money to and from various accounts, of which the client is not aware because it gets lost in the sea of numbers on the numerous pages sent to the client each month. Recently, someone who came to me for a consultation about their estate planning pointed to their statement and asked me what *"consults"* referred to. They were totally unaware of these moves or charges that the advisor was generating. They told me that when they later contacted the advisor about this issue, the advisor acted surprised with a "Who told you?" type of reaction. They immediately recognized the need for *godly* counsel. (Remember, you can get ungodly advice from a Christian.)

The only way to sometimes avoid these charges for exchanging money between accounts is to invest in what they often refer to as their *"core funds,"* which means either their own proprietary funds (funds owned and managed by or affiliated with the advisory company) or investment companies that they have a special arrangement with regarding management fees. Although it is usually better for the advisory firm and for the advisor that you invest in these "core funds," the question ought to be: Are these investments right for you? Too often that question is secondary to some advisors and their firms.

I have found that many firms have a "one size fits all" mentality. The advisor's advice is all too often not based on the best for the client but on what the most recent sales meetings were about. I have surprised many people (once they tell me the name of the firm with which they are working) by telling them what recommendations were already made to them, without me knowing what was said to them. It is important to remember that everyone's situation is different, and what might be right and good advice for one might be totally wrong for another, or at least not the best approach.

Another abuse using the platform approach is in the area of what we call "breakpoints." In recent years, the NASD (National Association of Securities Dealers) has been concerned with this area. Often an advisor will place your investment with a number of different investment companies, explaining that it is good to diversify among investment managers. While there is an element of truth in this, too many times he or she does so in order to maximize commissions by avoiding the breakpoint discounts investment companies offer for larger investments, which would reduce your costs in the placing and in the management of your investments. Breakpoints usually occur at set limits such as $50,000, $100,000 or $250,000 and even give you rights to accumulate to those amounts over a period of 13 months. It is interesting to note here that if you look into the portfolio holdings of the mutual funds with different investment companies they set up for diversification, oftentimes there is much overlap, discrediting their diversification argument.

I am my industry's biggest critic, as you may have guessed by now, and as I have said before, they often do things in ways that benefit themselves. The importance of your success often comes secondary to theirs. This is one of the reasons I started Cornerstone Financial Group, in order to provide biblical counsel independent of the pressures of quota-issuing advisory firms. It is our attempt to "come out from among them, and be ye separate" (2 Cor. 6:17 KJV). I would have done much better financially if I had followed their prescribed way of doing business, but their way is not always a reflection of God's way, which is what I am supposed to follow. We as Christians need to remember that we are the visible representation of Christ. The term *Christian* itself means "little Christ"!

Christian advisors from various firms have shared with me how they have been asked by their supervisors to move shares of a particular stock that the firm had in inventory due to the fact that the firm most likely underwrote the issue. One individual said that he was told by his manager that it was his responsibility to sell 10,000 shares of this particular stock to his clients. He responded by saying that he did not particularly like the stock, and that aside, he wasn't sure he had 10,000 shares worth of suitability among his clients. His manager simply repeated that it was his responsibility to move 10,000 shares of this particular stock among his clients while the title on his card proclaimed, "Financial Advisor."

Although this employee wanted to leave, he was prevented from doing so because his firm owned all the business he had produced, which meant that he would have to leave his clients behind. Some years before, he had fallen to the lure of cash and ego and the firm's appeal—"You are an awesome advisor and we want you to be part of our firm." Part of the contractual arrangement included his clients as property of the firm. What they really wanted was his assets under management; he was just an added benefit. He compromised and stayed because it would have been too much of a sacrifice to leave. Many firms have non-compete clauses in their contract preventing the advisor from taking his clients with him if he should go to another firm. After spending years building their business, advisors find themselves trapped by the sacrifices they would need to make if they left. If you are a new advisor (less than five years' experience) reading these words, you need to look at that contract you signed and seek God's plan for the future of your career.

It is not my purpose to write a "tell all" book about the financial advisory business, although that idea has been suggested to me. It *is* a great industry with a lot of good advisors and support people. My point is this: We need to be sure that we are seeking and receiving good and wise godly counsel. "Without counsel, plans go awry." Yep, that's in the Bible too! (See Proverbs 15:22a NKJV.) I have said before, that there are Christian advisors, and then there are advisors who are Christians. The first gives advice based on biblical principles, and the second gives advice from worldly institutions, either willingly or in ignorance of biblical principles. If you are an advisor reading this book, you too need to learn biblical principles so you can determine when you are giving biblical advice. Hey, I was once an advisor giving advice based on worldly principles taught to me by the financial institutions until the Lord began to show me His more excellent way! He made sure those old principles didn't work so well for me personally in order that I would seek out His plan.

I know what you are asking now: How do I choose an advisor? This is one of the most often-asked questions I hear when I am speaking. Here are some guidelines and some questions you might want to ask. This is how I would choose an advisor today.

1. *Is the advisor a believer?* This is of utmost importance. When I first broke into the business, I did not know another advisor who was a believer. It was a tough and worldly place for a young man to work. The industry was so destitute of believers that it made me question, as a young man, whether a believer was even to be in this business. However, I believe it was part of preparation for this time. Over the years God has been drawing more and more of His people into the advisory business. A number of them are associated with me in my practice. The initial problem is that many of these believing advisors are immediately drawn into the world's systems because they have been trained by the world, just as I was in the beginning. Your advisor must be *like minded* with you and *committed to advancing the Kingdom* with their business. It is very difficult to do estate planning with an individual who does not share your commitment to advancing the Kingdom by blessing vital ministries. He will not likely be enthusiastic about encouraging you to give, because that won't make him any money.

I do not believe that there is a place for a non-committed or unbelieving advisor in the planning process of a Christian. I have experienced myself and have had ministries inform me of Christians who were talked out of leaving an estate gift or gift of highly appreciated assets by their advisor, yes...even Christian ones! They apparently did not know Jesus' words about being "rich toward God" in Luke 12:21. Whose money is it? I think you know by now!

2. *Who are the people he respects and consults with?* This is probably the best test. *Choose someone who has a proven track record; has stood the test of time (this is the real-wheat-from-the-chaff sorter in this business); and has happy, satisfied, and...successful clients.* Interview the advisor if you do not know anything about him. Ask him about himself, his commitment to Christ, where he worships, his understanding of the Scriptures, his family situation, and business philosophy. Take notice of the pictures and items in his office. It will tell you a lot about him. Does he associate with Christian organizations or just industry organizations? The big question

to ask is, "Outside of your business, how are you helping to advance the Kingdom of Christ?" I have had "Christian" advisors tell me that they are just too busy with their business to work with Christians who need credit or budget counseling or to get involved with programs teaching biblical principles to the Body. Basically what they are saying is that their only interest is helping affluent Christians because it is the only thing that pays. I have met a number of advisors who hold up their faith in order to market to the Church.

3. *Don't be solely guided by awards or letters after his name.* Neither awards nor letters are good indications of a good or honest planner. Awards are usually given for accomplishing those things that the advisor's firm considers best for them, which usually means that the advisor used proprietary products (products sponsored by the firm). I have not received awards over the years even though I may have produced more overall production than those who did receive the awards, simply because I didn't use the products being promoted. Once, I far exceeded the production quota for a trip to Hawaii, but was not given the trip because I did not use the products they wanted me to use, whereas others, whose overall production was less, did receive the benefit. Why? I was guided instead by what best suited my client, and not by selling so much insurance, a certain number of shares of firm-sponsored funds, or stock. It is for this reason that for years I have shunned and not participated in awards programs offered by investment firms nor attended trips or conferences for which I qualified. I did not want anyone to question my motivation.

I think this type of activity reduces the level of professionalism in the industry. I have been embarrassed for the industry by advisors who flaunt, to their clients and the public, the trips they have won. This proves only that they are good salesmen, not good advisors. The industry has always catered to the egos of their agents or advisors. Many of my clients who come to me from other firms have described their previous advisors as self-impressed or "cocky." The industry itself fosters these types of attitudes, even while rewarding mediocrity. Earlier in my career, when I gained recognition for my "accomplishments," I remember throwing water unwittingly on the award ceremony when I laughingly asked why, if I had accomplished so much, I was still struggling to pay my bills, to which I received a rousing approval from the other advisors who were wondering the same thing.

The point is, the industry feeds the egos of the advisors to boost confidence and pride, in order to boost production. The problem is that when you feed something too much you create what I call "ego obesity." I remember a friend of mine, a Christian who is a manager in his firm, telling me how he had to cancel the contract of one of his best producers and ask him to leave. This man's ego had grown to such an extent that he considered everyone around him as a servant whom he treated most ungraciously. My friend said that despite the economic loss to him, he just had to do it, for his sake, the other employees' sakes, and the sake of the industry. I see these "ego obese" advisors all the time, even among Christians. You see, after nearly 30 years, I have learned to recognize the strut. Hey, there was a time when I strutted myself!

However, I have also learned that God does not use "strutting vessels," but "broken ones." Advisors, are you willing to allow yourself to become one of God's "cracked pots" and make the sacrifices in order to infect and affect the world for Christ in your practices?

Kingdom business does not always get you worldly recognition.

I was once called "peculiar" by a group of non-believing and non-committed Christian advisors I had been associated with. I considered it a compliment, because the Bible tells us that we are a "peculiar people" (see 1 Pet. 2:9, Titus 2:14, Deut. 26:18 KJV).

Do you want your advisor's recommendations driven by whether he or she will go to Hawaii or not?

I think not!

There are many advisors who also have an alphabet soup following their name, which simply means they have taken some courses. While many of the courses offered are excellent, the completion of such does not indicate whether the planner is good at what he does or, again most importantly, uses biblical principles. Even some of the popular letter designations adhere to non-biblical advice. (Work is underway and will be available shortly on a certification that designates a financial planner as a Christian who uses biblical principles.)

Let me try and give you a clear picture of the legal qualifications of an advisor.

These letters do not license anyone to do anything; only regulatory bodies and governmental authorities license and authorize people to give financial advice. These authorities do not produce any letters after your name, but provide a piece of paper legally recognizing your authority to act in prescribed manners. The actual word "license" is sometimes seen along with particular letter designations, but it is not referring to a governmental regulatory authorization; it simply refers to a license, authorization, or permission to use that designation. The people who use these letters play on the public's understanding of the word "license."

I once tried to train someone who had one of the most popular designations used in the industry today, after someone else in the firm had tried to do so and failed. The trainee had decided to take a course and get the designation before entering the financial advisory field. But because it licensed him to do nothing (it is not recognized by the state or NASD), he then had to take the state licensing courses to become registered. I too was unsuccessful in turning him into a good planner. He just didn't "get it," so he was let go. He now does fee-based planning on his own (advice only—he cannot help you get the financial products you need; he has no license or appointment to do so) and holds up this lettered designation as his qualification. If you need products, you need to get them yourself or go to someone else who does have the legal recognition to get them for you.

It is a requirement by the regulatory bodies that a licensed financial advisor must continue to stay up-to-date by achieving a certain number of continuing education credits in each licensing cycle. If he fails to do so, the license is suspended and eventually cancelled. Many of these courses do not lead to any lettered designation but are approved by the regulatory bodies. Some courses with designations can be used for this continuing education requirement, which is how I and many other experienced advisors have used these courses.

Many of these courses providing a designation have come about just over the last 20 years. The lettered designations have been developed by educational institutions and marketed to the financial professional.

They are in the business of selling educational services and they have done an excellent job. One such institution did a masterful job when it created a certain designation. Yes, they developed a good course, especially useful to new people starting out in the business, which gave them a solid background. The real credit to the success of this particular designation, however, was in the area of marketing.

They not only did a good job of marketing to the financial professional for continuing education credit, but they promoted it to the public as well, urging people to seek only those professionals with this designation. Consequently, the public began to ask advisors if they had this designation, and advisors began to seek it out. It was to the advisors' benefit to jump on the bandwagon. The marketing job caused the designation to outpace and become more recognized than a twice-as-stringent, older course and designation.

Again, I refer you to question #2 as the best way to find an advisor. It's the most reliable way. *Experience is the best teacher—experience that stands the test of time.* There are a number of advisors who, like me, have been around longer than some of the more popular designations have. We have watched them develop. I remember asking an excellent advisor I know who has been in the business almost as long as I have what he thought the difference was in him since he had completed one of the designations. He thought for a moment, and then laughed and replied, "I am $3,000 (the cost of the course) poorer!" He, like many of the older advisors (including me), past parts of the course without even opening the books. My point is…the courses are undeniably excellent—I encourage advisors to take them, but they are not and should not be the sole guiding principle as the course developers would like you to believe. Experience that stands the test of time is the best measure.

4. *Is **where** money is invested as important to the advisor as **how** it is invested?* This is real important to the committed Christian. I have said before that the Christian needs to *infect* the world in order to *affect* the world. *We must fill the world with our character, not allow its character to infiltrate us!* We have been commissioned in God's Word to promote God's plans and not to conform to the world's.

Many companies listed on the stock market today are striving to be politically correct instead of following guidelines laid down in God's Word for which they have no understanding or regard. In addition, there are also companies that profit from industries offensive to the believer, such as the pornography, abortion, alcohol, and tobacco industries. Then there are companies that support organizations and causes that are considered anti-family. I will not mention specific companies by name because I cannot change my printed words if a company should clean up its act in the future.

The National Association of Christian Financial Consultants (NACFC) maintains a current list of these companies known as the "Hall of Shame." On this list is an oil-producing company (most of you would not recognize the name) that is a major part of some of the most widely held mutual funds. This particular company also happens to be in partnership with a genocidal African government that is responsible for the routine slaughter and enslavement of many of our brothers and sisters in Christ.

Do you want this company as part of your portfolio?

No, we don't! Yet many ministry retirement programs are invested in mutual funds that are invested in this company's stock.

Then there are the obvious companies, one of which produces medical supplies for abortion procedures. (Ironically, this company also produces a large line of baby products.) Some companies make the "Hall of Shame" list because of their giving patterns. Even though their products may not be offensive, they themselves are major contributors to the gay and lesbian lifestyle. We as Christians love these individuals, but we cannot condone a lifestyle that is declared by God in Leviticus chapter 18 to be an "abomination." We must love the homosexual, but we cannot support a lifestyle that stands in opposition to God.

Today, we have the capability to screen mutual funds to determine the number of biblical violations that are committed in relationship to the particular mutual fund. My question is: How much money can we invest into things contrary to Scripture? I say nothing!

Also included on the Hall of Shame list are some investment advisory firms, one which I find many Christians working with simply because they do not know about the issues they support. This firm advertises that they have more advisors with one of the most popular designations we just talked about than any other firm.

Hmm...what does that tell you again about a Christian using designations as the sole reason for choosing an advisor?

Some advisors will tell you that it is not possible to invest without violations. They are telling you this for one of two reasons:

1. They don't know that it can be done, or

2. Their firm considers it politically incorrect to attempt to invest without violations, and will not contract to allow their advisors to do this. However, they do not want to lose your business, so they compromise.

I remember meeting with an individual who was also a board member of a Christian organization that employed a number of people. When I told him about the ability to screen and provide investments that were morally responsible, he appeared stunned. He related to me how they had just put a retirement program in place for the employees of an organization where the employees had requested these particular types of investments. The advisor, a well-known and respected man in the Christian community, told them it was not possible to do such a thing. He then had them install a program using an investment company that is considered one of the worst violators. The truth is, he would not have been able to introduce the other program because his firm would not make morally responsible investments available to him.

In February 2004, *Forbes Magazine* carried an article entitled, "Holy Influence," that featured my friend Art Ally, the founder of the Timothy Plan (named after the Book of Timothy in the Bible). The Timothy Plan had recently caught Forbes' attention because of their success, performance, and in particular, the war they had waged with Wal-Mart regarding that company's decision to sell pornography in their stores. The Timothy Plan, a stockholder in Wal-Mart placed the company on the "Hall of Shame" list and instructed their money managers to liquidate all shares of the company's stock from their holdings. I was traveling a lot during the month that this issue came out on the stands, and I enjoyed seeing that magazine with the picture of Art in it everywhere I went.

Why?

Because my vision and dream (as well as Art's and others), of seeing Christians finally *infecting* and *affecting* the world through investments that God has entrusted to them, was coming to reality. It has been hard to beat this drum for years wondering if anyone has been listening, and then, finally, behold...evidence that it is working! The Timothy Plan, a family of mutual funds has been growing rapidly in recent years as more of God's people have become aware of the opportunity to invest according to biblical principles. These funds are managed by top-ranked money managers who are kept up-to-date with information on those companies that they must not allow in their portfolio. This screening does not affect performance since the offending companies are a small percentage overall. The Timothy Plan is the only morally responsible fund based on biblical principles that has zero tolerance for any biblical violations within its investment portfolio.

I am still amazed, as are other NACFC advisors, at how many advisors and investors, when made aware of the opportunity to invest with biblical principles, ask, "What's the return?" While the subject of return is important, and this particular return happens to be comparable to other funds, they have still missed the point. I know of an individual who passed on the opportunity to invest in the Timothy Plan because he had not heard of the fund company and instead invested according to the advice of a popular Christian newsletter in a fund which at the time had 53-percent violations. (That's $53 out of every $100 invested in things offensive to the Christian.)

What's wrong with this picture?

Is your faith a commitment or a preference?

Planning and conducting a financial life according to God's standards is simply not a priority for some Christians or for some believing advisors as well. I know—I used to be one of them! They have not caught hold of the vision...*yet!* But I'm believing for you folks to join us in this revolution.

If you are an advisor signing on to the revolution, let us know by indicating so when you sign the induction papers at the back of this book. Then seed into this effort by giving copies of this book to your clients. Help us spread the word!

If you need a referral to an advisor, let us know this as well when you send in your induction papers, and we will work with the NACFC to find one in your area.

Another question I often hear is whether you should use a fee-based planner or a commission-based planner. The talking heads (who, by the way, are not licensed individuals, for licensed individuals are not able to give generalized advice) on TV and on radio financial shows will tell you to seek these individuals because they give unbiased advice, and this may be true. Many fee-based planners are not licensed to handle any products so they cannot help with implementation.

The answer really depends on the one using the service. The best advice is, once you have followed the four points listed above, find some-one who can accept a fee or a commission, and who is not motivated by proprietary products (investments named after and managed by their advisory firm). It is usually cheaper for most clients to use commission-based, unless it is a one-time consultation with someone for a specific reason (i.e., estate planning). Contrary to what people think, fee-based commissions charged for financial planning and investment management usually end up being more expensive in the long run, because you must continue to pay fees out of your pocket (usually deducted from your account) on an ongoing basis for as long as you use the service.

Uh-oh, here I go flirting with that "tell-all" book again!

Let me state again that the financial advisory business is a good industry, full of good people, offering good advice; but I think it necessary to caution you of some things, only so that those of you who do not know the industry can have a better understanding and can make good decisions regarding who you should accept advice from. Be aware that the industry does have some self-seeking "bad apples," and you need to be careful.

When the public began to demand fee-based planners, I remember saying something I used to say to the kids I worked with at a residential treatment center…"Be careful what you ask for; you just might get it!" I knew that what the public was seeking could ultimately be more expensive in the long run.

While the media promoted the idea of fee-based planning, organizations began to pop up offering advisors assistance in switching their practice from commission based to fee based, in order to meet the public cry for this type of advisor. I remember seeing a cartoon in one of the industry trade magazines picturing two guys in a commission-based practice, desks piled high with service work (for which they did not receive any compensation) watching the fee-based guy across the hall leaving with his golf clubs, and wondering how he did it. While writing this chapter, I received the following communication, which tells the whole story. I assure you I did not make it up! I copied and pasted it into my manuscript, and I quote it exactly as I received it, but will not identify the source, for obvious legal reasons, and because I don't wish to embarrass anyone who should be embarrassed. It reads…

"Dear Buck,

I know *you've been thinking about moving into fee-based planning…*

Good Lord, who isn't?

After all, it's the single hottest trend in the planning industry!

In fact, *it's the perfect business* for 2005 and beyond!

A business where you *create a huge residual income,* one that will continue for years and years to come. One where deep-pocketed investors will throw wheelbarrows of cash at you…bidding each other up in an attempt to get you to consult with them.

Let's face it—if you are an agent or rep…

You won't get paid bupkus for your commission-based practice. Even after slaving for years to build it up!

However, **build a fee-based practice** and after just three to five years you will **have hordes of confused investors banging down your door** to get your financial advice...IF you present yourself correctly!

Positioned properly, you can have a business that will set you up for life in as little as 12 to 18 months."

What a bunch of baloney! I read it and felt like vomiting! How unprofessional! They embarrass the industry by trying to sell their services to non-fee based planners, appealing to their greed.

Advisors, this kind of stuff cheapens our integrity and industry! We are supposed to be professionals!

I share this correspondence with you hoping it will cause you to seek godly counsel from someone who is motivated by advancing the Kingdom, and not by greed and building up a business that will "set him up for life." I would much rather be about the work that will set me up for abundant life in Christ and eventually eternal life! I want God's people to be set free from the worldly systems and its entrapments, and that includes worldly advisors.

Let me summarize my thoughts about selecting an advisor by restating point number 2:

Choose a committed Christian advisor who has a proven track record; has stood the test of time (this is the real-wheat-from-the-chaff sorter in this business); and has happy, satisfied, and...*successful* clients. Choose an advisor who is concerned about *how* the money is invested and *where* it is invested, and who will not only advise you but help you implement your plan as well. He or she should also be willing to be compensated in a manner (fee or transaction) that is best for you.

I do not recommend that you do your own financial planning any more than I suggest that you wire the electricity in your own house (if you're not an electrician). You need to be sure that things are properly grounded and that you do not get things crossed up. Reading a book might help you somewhat, but just as with electrical wiring, it's best to call a professional. Your own plan may seem to be right and good, but there may be some situations of which you are not aware, that are not the safest or best thing for you. There are definitely some pitfalls of which you need to avoid; and a godly and qualified advisor can definitely be an asset as you set God's financial plan for your life.

Closely related to financial planning is estate planning, and in light of the times, this is an area the Church must concentrate on. Come with me to the next chapter where we will discuss estate planning!

CHAPTER 15

ESTATE PLANNING

Estate planning is an area that most people have neglected, especially Christians. Many people think that if they have a written will, they are set. That may be true if you do not have any assets to distribute, and the only thing you need to do is appoint an executor to close out your estate. But in fact, most people in the United States do not even have a will. We need to realize, however, that those who have accumulated substantial assets need to do a little more in-depth planning. The senior generation today is the wealthiest generation to have ever lived! These people have seen incredible increases in the value of their real estate as well as incredible growth in their income. Blue-collar workers are retiring today as millionaires due to the growth inside their retirement programs and the growth of their property values. They don't think of themselves as wealthy, so they neglect to do anything about it.

Listen to me. If we do not decide, the government will! The government has set up estate taxes for the purpose of redistributing the wealth (by first going through their hands, of course). We are learning firsthand what Jeremiah meant when he said in Lamentations 5:2: "Our inheritance has been turned over to aliens, and our homes to foreigners." However, through proper planning, you can decide (hopefully under the Spirit's direction) how that money is to be used, and let us not forget whose money it is! How does God want you to use it?

Perhaps you feel that you don't have an estate tax problem. Do you have sizeable amounts of money in qualified (that means money which has not been taxed yet) retirement accounts, such as an IRA, 401K or 403B (TSA) program? If you do, you have another type of tax problem! One you most likely will pass on to your heirs. And no one likes to inherit a tax problem. I won't get into the details or the how-to's here; that is not the purpose of this book. However, I encourage you to contact us at the address in the back of the book for more details on this type of problem.

Whether you have a tax problem or not, how do you plan to distribute your wealth, especially if you have assets of any size, when you leave this world?

In First Timothy 6:17-20a, Paul charges the Christian to have eternal values in mind when considering personal finances. He is commanded to be generous and willing to share, for in so doing, he will have true treasure. Let's listen while the Apostle Paul talks to Pastor Timothy:

> *Command those who are rich in this present world not to be arrogant nor to put their hope in wealth, which is so uncertain, but to put their hope in God, who richly provides us with everything for our enjoyment. Command them to do good, to be rich in good deeds, and to be generous and willing to share. In this way they will lay up treasure for themselves as a firm foundation for the coming age, so that they may take hold of the life that is truly life. Timothy, guard what has been entrusted to your care.*

Let's review again. How does the Christian gain true riches that can be used in the coming age? He does so by investing in the Kingdom, giving his or her money to efforts that advance the Kingdom of Jesus Christ! God commands us not only to use our wealth for our own good and the good of our family, but to take advantage of every opportunity to be generous, and to do so with eternal values in view. You see, we are not only to give gifts out of current income, but to continue our giving through our estates with gifts to ministries!

The great Bible commentator, Matthew Henry, in his comments on this passage says, "The Christian must be charged to think of another world and to prepare for that which is to come by works of charity."

In my experience, *material prosperity without righteous application, leads to spiritual dullness, sin, and often a loss of that prosperity!*

Read that last sentence again!

God believes in the redistribution-of-*His*-wealth principle, and He encourages us to take care of our own. In Second Corinthians 12:14, Paul says, "Children should not have to save up for their parents, but parents for their children." He encourages us to redistribute our wealth not only to our children, but also, as we have seen, to "lay up treasures in Heaven." We do that by investing that wealth He has given us into His Kingdom, *to invest it in the harvest of souls!*

Investing in souls!

Now there is something you won't see listed on the stock exchange! But let me tell you, the return on that investment is incredible! It lasts for eternity, and it is *guaranteed!*

What then should the goals be in our estate planning? Following are, what I believe, five major goals for the Christian, based on Scripture:

1. To preserve our estate for our heirs.

2. To reduce taxation or redistribution of the wealth as determined by the government.

3. To provide for an orderly settlement of our estate at our death.

4. To generously bless ministries that are dedicated to advancing the Kingdom of Jesus Christ.

5. To continue to affect the world for Christ even though we have departed.

Many people will leave their entire estate to their children, which often creates problem situations. In fact, if parents would have had the ability to see into the future, they would have chosen to direct their estate in different areas. Over the years, I have watched inheritances squandered, the effect of tax liabilities that burdened the surviving children to such an extent that they were forced to sell a business or assets that they would rather not have sold, and family disputes erupting out of control, all because of the lack of detailed planning. I am sure that the parents would have never guessed that after their death, their children would behave as they did.

I remember a few years ago being involved in the settlement of an estate of a woman who was in the 50-percent tax bracket at the time. Even though she thought she had left everything to her children, in reality, only 50 percent went to her children; the other 50 percent went to the government. She had only a will—no trusts or any tax planning. The final item to settle was her home, and the best offer on the home was $20,000 less than the minimum the four children had decided they would take. House sales were difficult at the time, and I called them in for counseling. I pointed out to them that even though they wanted $20,000 more than the offer, if they waited, they would only net $10,000 after taxes with $10,000 going to the IRS. I then said to them, "Let's put this into perspective; there are four of you, and $10,000 divided by four equals $2,500. The question I pose to each of you is this: Do you want to risk losing this offer and possibly wait awhile longer for $2,500?" Immediately, they saw that the additional $20,000 meant only $2,500 more for each of them, and they decided to accept the offer.

There has been some tax changes since the time of that case, lessening the burden on the estate; but the point is—even though a very large sum of money went to the children, a very large sum also went to the IRS. If this woman had simply done some estate planning, she could have decided to give that money to a ministry rather than the IRS. If you were forced to write a check either to the IRS or to a ministry that you support, which would you do? I do not think many of you would choose the IRS! Remember whose money it will become if you don't decide. The IRS thinks of your money as theirs! Theirs, in this case, is spelled t-h-e-IRS!

You may have that decision staring you in the face; seriously consider that if you do not choose where you want your money to go, your Uncle Sam will! Maybe he will send it to buy a $10,000 screwdriver for the defense department. They have proven themselves in the past to be poor money managers. The government is made up of people like us, who have not been trained in money management and who do not employ biblical principles in their decisions. This is why taxes have continued to rise over the years and the deficit has increased. More money and more debt increases will not eliminate the financial problem in the government—the same thing happening in the average American home and unfortunately among those who should know better...the Church!

"Buck, are you saying that if we have substantial assets, we should not leave them all to our children?" No, I am not saying that. I am saying that the Bible indicates that we should not only take care of our children but that we are to also invest in the Kingdom. We must do both!

This is not simply my opinion. I believe we have a clear mandate from Scripture. I also believe from firsthand experience with people who have inherited wealth, that we may be doing more harm than good by indulging our children too much.

Here are some quotes of the wealthy, which may shed some light on how we think about this subject:

For a person of wealth to think of handing it down to a child is almost like handing down a gun. Inherited wealth does more harm than good...it eats away at your self-esteem. More people resent you than admire you. You never know who is approaching you for what agenda.

Swanee Hunt, daughter of H.L. Hunt
(*Parade* magazine, November 1997)

[The perfect inheritance] is enough money so that they feel they could do anything, but not so much that they could do nothing!

Warren Buffett, (*Fortune*, September 1986)

Because we love you very much, we have decided not to leave you a lot of money. [That must have gone over the dinner table like a lead balloon.]

Joseph Jacobs to his children (Forbes, May 1997)

The only thing you get to keep is that which you give away.

Edwin Kennedy, former managing director
and CEO of Lehman Brothers
(These words were spoken to me in a fishing
boat on Owasco Lake in New York, 1992)

Whoever loves money never has money enough; whoever loves wealth is never satisfied with his income. This too is meaningless. As goods increase, so do those who consume them. And what benefit are they to the owner, except to feast his eyes on them?

Solomon, the richest man of all time,
1000 B.C. (Ecclesiates 5:10-11)

There is an old adage in estate planning, and it goes like this:

The first generation makes the wealth; the second generation retains the wealth; the third generation spends the wealth; and the fourth generation starts again!

How true, how true! Talk to financial advisors and attorneys who have worked with families like this. I have seen it a number of times in my practice where the wealth of the family quickly slips away in the hands of a generation unprepared to handle it.

The Christian's attitude should be to provide opportunity but not a lifestyle when considering their estate plans and providing for their heirs. I think Warren Buffet's suggestion above is excellent advice. Provide opportunity, and for the Christian, the surplus should be invested in the Kingdom.

Jesus, the Master, in Luke 12:21 gave His redistribution-of-wealth principle and said that anyone who lays up treasure for himself or herself "and is not rich toward God" is a fool. Why a fool? Think of the crowns that he or she is giving up in the Kingdom. *This is the only way you can take something of value from your estate with you when you die!* Do not give up that return on the Master's mina!

With an estate investment in the Kingdom, you can continue to earn "crowns" even after you are gone!

How much have you sent on ahead? How many souls have you invested in?

Edwin Kennedy gave away millions when he was alive and also when he died. His investments then are continuing to earn him crowns even now after he is gone. Remember what he said to me: *"The only thing you get to keep is that which you give away."* How true. How biblical!

That is financial faithfulness! That is stewardship! That is obedience! That is being like Christ! As the martyred missionary Jim Elliot said, "He is no fool who gives what he cannot keep, to gain what he cannot lose." He made the ultimate investment; his faith was a commitment, not a preference!

Why is estate planning in the church so important? The senior generation is a generation of wealth, the wealthiest generation to have ever lived. It is estimated by the financial industry that 7 to 10 trillion dollars will pass to the next generation (the baby boomers) in the next five to ten years! It is also estimated that the number of millionaires will increase in the United States. It is also estimated and very probable that 20 to 30 percent of that money is now in the hands of believers. Think of the potential here! We will visit this again when we consider the vision of the financially faithful Church.

CHAPTER *16*

CHURCH DEBT

C hurch debt is an area that causes many congregational debates. Let me start by saying that church borrowing has been necessitated by the disobedience of our forefathers as well as our own disobedience in the area of finances. God tells us in Deuteronomy 28 that His plan for His people is to be the lender, not the borrower. Church borrowing is not sin; it is just not God's preferred way. What I am saying is that when following God's plan, we should not have to borrow, or at least not borrow outside the church. So with that in mind, let's take a look at this issue.

Many of our churches today are debt free, but many others carry mortgage balances. Over the years, churches have proven to be good credit risks to lenders, and lenders usually have no problem making loans to established churches, although new and independent churches are considered more carefully.

In my experience I have seen churches develop strong cash flows in order to support a corporate debt and to make monthly payments for new buildings or expansions. There was even a time when I used to assist churches in obtaining the necessary financing to expand or build, and I was very skilled at it! But if the Bible tells us that "the borrower is the servant to the lender" (Prov. 22:7), then what should our attitude be about churches borrowing money?

I am asked this question so often it is amazing. There are many people who believe it is perfectly fine for a church to mortgage its property. There are also many other people who believe it is in direct violation of the Scriptures. The Spirit has often led me to respond this way to this very controversial subject in the church: The church must seek to do what God leads. Proverbs 22:7 says, "The rich rule over the poor, and the borrower is the servant to the lender." Church leaders must ask themselves this question first before attempting to raise money through credit: "Do I, as a church leader, desire to put this property, which belongs to the Master, into servitude to a secular worldly institution?"

Now, that is a tough question, and I do not wish to condemn or indict any institution one way or the other in this matter, nor do I believe that borrowing is sin, but let us look at some issues that surround this question.

First, borrowing is credit. Credit's purpose is to help you get something for which you do not yet have the money. The Master in the parable of the ten minas did not tell His servants to go and borrow from others using His property as collateral. He gave them something to start with and told them to multiply it and then bring it back to Him.

Second, borrowing denies you, as a servant of the Master, the opportunity to experience His blessings in response to your giving. God's provision in this way, will not only build your faith, but will be a witness to the community. I recall a community where two new churches were built about the same time. People from the community described both churches as beautiful structures, but the one they were particularly impressed with was the one that the people were building debt free. The world's expectations fall far short of those kind of accomplishments—great things being accomplished through the faith and the faithfulness of God's people. It was also interesting to note that a couple of years later, the level of prosperity of the church and the individuals who gave sacrificially to the construction of the church had increased! Remember, *prosperity* and *obedience* in the Bible are the same word!

I once conducted an Advancing the Kingdom Weekend at a church filled with ordinary, everyday children of God. Their new building plans were on the wall when we arrived, and their bank financing was in place. I remember the Spirit prompted me in the middle of the Sunday morning sermon to speak to them about who they are in Christ. I had just spent the weekend teaching biblical financial principles, and the next week, their people began attending the Crown small group study. At no time had I suggested that they build debt free, but as they studied the Word on the subject of finances, they caught the vision and decided at the Spirit's prompting to trust God and begin building. What happened thereafter was miraculous. One and a half years later, we were invited to their new building dedication, a building built by faith and debt free—not by ordinary people, but by children of God, joint heirs with Christ, special people walking in faith and faithfulness, believing the Word of God!

Third, a debt in the church can restrict the church and its members in service to the Master. Decisions regarding the finances of the church may be based on meeting debt requirements instead of the program needs of the church. Add up the annual interest of your church's debt and then ask yourself, "What could God do with that money? How else could it be spent here?" That is a real eye-opener. The devil also uses debt to cause divisions among the people of the church and church leadership.

Fourth, I have seen many lenders require the signature of personal guarantee from the pastor who may be viewed by them as the glue that holds the church together. This restricts his ability to be free to serve the Master because he must remain as pastor during the term of the loan. I do not believe any church should allow this type of arrangement. The pastor is personally guaranteeing the ability of the membership to repay the loan. Is this a step of faith on his part, or is it co-signing? By definition, it is the latter, which is definitely prohibited by Scripture.

In Scripture, there are three instances where a place of worship was built, and I would like to use two as examples that I believe God would have us to consider.

To begin with, in Deuteronomy 8:18, God said that the ability to accumulate wealth is a confirmation of the covenant that He made with us. This means, if we follow biblical principles (obedience), then we will accumulate wealth (prosperity). Then in Deuteronomy 28:12, God told the people through Moses that they would lend to many nations and borrow from none. This directive by God is evidenced in Exodus 25:1-2 NASU where God instructed Moses to "Tell the Israelites to *raise* a contribution for Me," according to how their heart was moved in preparation for the building of the tabernacle. Then in Exodus 36, Moses issued a proclamation that no further contributions were needed; all was paid for and the tabernacle was built debt free.

In First Chronicles chapter 29, David declared that Solomon was to build the temple and that it was to be built from the "abundance" that had been provided by God. One of the most magnificent structures of all time was built in Jerusalem debt free! People, as part of the preparation process, brought offerings; others donated time and materials prior to and during the construction. And many churches over the years have been built this way. It has only been in the 20th century that "financing" a church has become the norm.

Financing is the "American way," and it has crept into the church because we have not been obedient over the years in handling money God's way. We have become the borrower and not the lender. (God is about to change that...you'll see...read on!)

When a church is first founded, the contributions for the church building are usually collected immediately. So often, however, when a church plans an expansion, many plans are made before any consideration of how to pay for it is made. With the need at hand, and the plans made, it is standard then to approach the bank. I have been involved in that type of effort and never gave it a second thought; it was the normal thing to do in America! Never thought twice about it until the Lord Himself prompted me to consider the Scriptures and the precedents set in God's Word.

My dear friend Vyrl Pember, who founded Church Financial Development in Tulsa, Oklahoma, pastored for a number of years. The Lord spoke to him about church debt when he began pastoring a large church with a $2-million debt. Vyrl then launched a campaign (which is a lot more than just taking pledges) and led that church as they paid off their mortgage. The program was so effective that other churches began to ask him to guide them in paying off their mortgages or raising expansion capital. Since that time, he has assisted many ministries in raising an offering to eliminate or avoid church debt. So you see, even if your church has mortgaged their property, you can still become debt free by raising the money to pay the mortgage early.

Over the years as a consultant to a number of different ministries, I have concluded that debt is an enemy to church unity. It should be eliminated or avoided wherever possible.

I am also a believer that the "chickens will die off to the size of the hen coop." So what do you do if you do not yet have the money to increase the size of the hen coop? I say, if you must borrow to accommodate the chickens, do not be satisfied to sit back and amortize the loan. Start a program to retire the debt as early as possible.

I know that this view is not popular with a number of my brothers and sisters in the Lord. I must agree that financing does make expansion seem easier and perhaps earlier, but our God is a God of miracles, not of convenience. He is not a God of ministerial instant gratification! He is more interested in our growth than in our comfort. When a leader leads the church into a debt-free existence, he or she must step out of their comfort zone, and that is called faith! It's not blind faith though, because your eyes are on the Word!

The leaders of a church must consider all the alternatives before putting the church into the servitude of debt (see Prov. 22:7). If they must do so anyway, because of real need, then they need to pursue eliminating that servitude as soon as possible.

My conviction is this: If we teach the people of the church to handle money in biblical ways (how the Bible tells us to handle the 90 percent as well as the 10 percent), then over time, the need to borrow will go away. We will become what I call the Kingdom Bank!

PART 3

CALL TO ARMS

CHAPTER 17

THE ULTIMATE IDENTITY THEFT

I dentity theft, a form of forgery where someone steals another's legal identity for illicit purposes, has become an ever growing problem in our society. We all seem to have either experienced it or know of someone who has been violated by someone else using their social security number, credit card numbers, or other forms of legal identity to purchase, charge, or withdraw money in the violated person's name, without their knowledge.

My wife, Andrea, was involved with a situation of identity theft in 2002, while working in the retail furniture business. A man masquerading as another man purchased a large amount of furniture, successfully financing it in the name of this other man from another state whom he did not know, but whose personal information he had illegally obtained. The police became involved when the real man reported that he had not bought any furniture, nor had he ever been to the city where my wife worked.

The whole ordeal began to unravel when Andrea recognized the thief's picture in the newspaper and informed the appropriate authorities. The police were stunned by her information, and they began to investigate further, discovering that this man was wanted in eight states for an elaborate scheme of identity theft. Everything he possessed, he had purchased as a result of stealing another's authority and identity. The furniture he had bought from my wife was found in his apartment and was eventually returned to the store. Guess what my wife's reward was for reporting the tip to the police? She was to return the commissions earned on the sale of the furniture. Everyone lost!

Still, she credits the unraveling of this elaborate scheme to the fact that she said to this man, as she did to so many customers, "God bless you." She believes, as I do, that stopping this man from his escalating criminal activity was the best form of blessing God could bestow on him at that time.

This problem is one that we would do well to protect ourselves from, not only by protecting our legal identity bestowed on us by society, but in an even bigger way.

You see, identity theft is a significant and growing problem for the Church today, to those who name Jesus Christ as their Lord and Savior, and yet, it is not a new problem. Identity theft dates all the way back to before the Garden of Eden, when lucifer, the great counterfeiter himself tried to steal God's identity, thinking he could be like God.

> *How art thou fallen from heaven, O lucifer, son of the morning! How art thou cut down to the ground, which didst weaken the nations! For thou hast said in thine heart, I will ascend into heaven, I will exalt my throne above the stars of God: I will sit also upon the mount of the congregation, in the sides of the north: I will ascend above the heights of the clouds:* **I will be like the most High.** *Yet thou shalt be brought down to hell, to the sides of the pit* (Isaiah 14:12-15 KJV, emphasis added).

Think of this…

If satan thought he could steal God's identity, do you think he might also try to steal yours?

The fact is, he did not steal God's identity but instead was cast out of Heaven. However, he then, given the chance, approached Adam and Eve, who did allow him to steal their identity. They had been given dominion, but they ceased to act like those with authority. Eventually, they ran and hid from God because of their sin.

Now, let me ask you this…

Who do you think planted that seed of the tree of the knowledge of good and evil in the Garden of Eden?

God?

I don't think so.

Consider this! James 1:13-14 tells us that God does not tempt us.

*Let no man say when he is tempted, I am tempted of God: for God cannot be tempted with evil, **neither tempteth He any man**: but every man is tempted, when he is drawn away of his own lust, and enticed* (KJV, emphasis added).

The tree of knowledge of good and evil represented the temptation before Adam and Eve to disobey God. For many years, I believed that God had put the tree there to test His creation.

Then one day…

The Holy Spirit said to me, "I did not plant that tree!"

I said, "Of course, You did, Lord. Who else would have?"

He then pointed me to James 1:13-14 and told me that if He indeed tempted anyone, they would be unable to resist His temptation because He, God, cannot fail in any effort. He said, "If I tempted you, you would submit to the temptation. You would be unable to withstand. But remember, it is I who provides the way of escape from that temptation." (See First Corinthians 10:13.)

I understood what He was saying. He went on to explain that He sowed good seed in the garden of the earth, but the enemy who had been cast out of Heaven down to the earth, came and sowed tares among the good seed. "Hey, Lord," I said, "that sounds familiar." It did sound familiar to me, and I recognized it as the "Parable of the Sower."

Jesus presented another parable to them, saying, "The kingdom of heaven may be compared to a man who sowed good seed in his field. But while his men were sleeping, his enemy came and sowed tares among the wheat, and went away. But when the wheat sprouted and bore grain, then the tares became evident also. The slaves of the landowner came and said to him, 'Sir, did you not sow good seed in your field? How then does it have tares?' And he said to them, 'An enemy has done this!' The slaves said to him, 'Do you want us, then, to go and gather them up?' But he said, 'No; for while you are gathering up the tares, you may uproot the wheat with them. Allow both to grow together until the harvest; and in the time of the harvest I will say to the reapers, "First gather up the tares and bind them in bundles to burn them up; but gather the wheat into my barn" ' " (Matthew 13:24-30 NASU).

Then after a few verses, Jesus explained this parable to His disciples further...

Then He left the crowds and went into the house. And His disciples came to Him and said, "Explain to us the parable of the tares of the field." And He said, "The one who sows the good seed is the Son of Man, and the field is the world; and as for the good seed, these are the sons of the kingdom; and the tares are the sons of the evil one; **and the enemy who sowed them is the devil,** *and the harvest is the end of the age; and the reapers are angels. So just as the tares are gathered up and burned with fire, so shall it be at the end of the age. The Son of Man will send forth His angels, and they will gather out of His kingdom all stumbling blocks, and those who commit lawlessness, and will throw them into the furnace of fire; in that place there will be weeping and gnashing of teeth. Then THE RIGHTEOUS WILL SHINE FORTH AS THE SUN in the kingdom of their Father. He who has ears, let him hear"* (Matthew 13:36-43 NASU, emphasis added).

Hmm. I "thunk" about this hard and long.

Yes, "thunk" is a word...I made it up! "Thunk" is a much deeper sound, denoting deeper thought and meaning than "think" or "thought" (my definition). It indicates my deep consideration, thought, and pondering of a subject. So you see...*I "thunk" about this and realized that the devil had access to the garden prior to the fall (he was there to tempt Adam and Eve before they sinned), and ever since, the enemy has been continuously sowing tares in the garden of our lives.* Why? He wants to deceive us into disobedience. He wants what God has given us as joint heirs with Christ, that's why! He wants our authority! He wants our identity!

You see, this is a disempowering tool the devil uses to paralyze us. The believer is often unsuccessful in his finances or in other areas of life because he simply does not know who he is! He does not have a vision of himself as God sees him. He forgets that the devil is under his feet; he is not under the devil's feet (see Luke 10:19).

When I was speaking at a church one weekend, Andrea said to me, "They are such precious people, but they do not know who they are!" I remember during the Sunday morning services while I was giving the message, the Spirit suddenly had me stop and ask, "Do you people know who you are?" I then left the intended direction of my message to talk to them about who they are in Christ. Their identity and vision of who they are had been stolen, and they did not recognize the authority they had been given to accomplish great things. This group of people did catch hold of the vision, regained their identity, and two years later had accomplished great things in the Lord. They decided to not draw down on a construction loan and ended up building their new building debt free! They accomplished the unthinkable! We would call them average working people, but you see God calls them "sons and daughters"!

How did these precious people and the church at large forget who they are? How does the devil sow tares into our lives and steal our identity? Let's look at some of the ways he connivingly works to take what does not belong to him.

1. SATAN CONVINCES US TO TELL OURSELVES LIES.

Satan is very subtle. At the enemy's prompting, God's people will tell themselves lies, such as: "I'm no good...I cannot do anything right!...I'm ugly...I am no good with money...I will never amount to anything...I am not as good as others...I have no gifts, no talent, and nothing to offer the church...I am not deserving of God's favor...I will never have my own home...I have made too many mistakes, surely God can't forgive me...I am not smart enough...I am just an average person, what can I do?...I do not have the opportunity...I am the product of my environment...I am destined to live this way...It's my parent's fault!...It's society's fault...I can never do anything right...I feel like God doesn't love me..."

Need I go on? You get the idea. Perhaps you have repeated some of these same things and could add some enemy-inspired, identity-crushing statements to this list. This type of thinking keeps us paralyzed and prevents us from becoming all that God has purposed for our lives. The enemy is quick to provide us excuses as to why we are not successful or achieving all that God has purposed in His heart for us. The unfortunate fact is that many of us never achieve what God has for us because we believe the lies satan has us tell ourselves. He tells us these lies, and then he keeps repeating them so that we say them to ourselves over and over and over until we believe them. The biggest enemy to our success and living the abundant life Jesus promised, is ourselves and our "stinkin' thinkin'." How did these lies get into our heads in the first place?

The enemy sent someone or something to sow tares into the garden of our mind, where God intended to grow the "mind of Christ" (see 1 Cor. 2:16).

2. SATAN SENDS OTHERS TO TELL US LIES.

It seems that from the time we are born, the enemy marks those whom he senses are called to a higher purpose. His strategy is detestable because he often uses those closest to us, those who have the greatest influence in our lives to plant seeds of inferiority, negativity, failure, and poor self-concept into our lives. So many of us struggle with believing that God has a purpose and a high calling for our lives because of the lies that have been spoken to us and over us from the earliest of our days. Comments and statements from parents, relatives, teachers, classmates, coaches, employers, and sometimes even our spouses can affect how we feel about ourselves and cause us not to see ourselves as God sees us, stealing our God-given identity. Even pastors, church leaders, and other believers can have a negative impact on our lives. This is so sad, but it is true.

So many people have been driven from the church and into a state of identity theft because of a judgmental or controlling spirit projected from church leaders and brothers and sisters in Christ who do not speak the truth in love but in a spirit of judgment or a holier-than-thou attitude. Even a pastor can have an abusive and controlling spirit towards his flock, attempting to manipulate and control them. God forbid if they leave that church, for these pastors will also get others to shun them, a form of emotional and spiritual abuse contributing to their negative self-worth and lack of effectiveness in the Kingdom.

Am I speaking to any leaders out there? I know I am!

Yes, even in the Church in America are those who abuse a high calling for their own purposes. God will eventually remove these leaders, and obedient church leaders will then need to deal with their collateral damage! We must recognize that sometimes just because someone is in the ministry, does not mean they have been "called." I am amazed at the people I find who have been emotionally and spiritually abused because of a church relationship.

Yep, tares in the church! There is no place that the devil does not sow tares. Often these church leaders are people who have had their identity stolen as well.

"You will never amount to anything!...Can't you do anything right?...Why can't you be like so-and-so?...You're just not a good student." These identity-stealing statements spoken by others (as well as those previously listed), coupled with the emotional, mental, and physical abuse that often accompanies these lies, have left so many of us scarred and ineffective in the Kingdom. Believe it or not, this is not God's perfect plan for our lives or how He sees any of us. Remember, "God don't make no junk!" This is more than just a funny statement. God truly does not make anything just for kicks! *God conducts no experiments!* He knows exactly what results He is going to get. You are not a biochemical accident, nor did you slither out of a puddle and start to learn calculus as the evolutionists try to tell us. God knows exactly what He is doing! He has a purpose and a high calling for each of us...Oh yes, He does!

Just because someone has said something about you or treated you in a way that reduced your feelings of self-worth, does not make it so. You may not have been born, grew up, or even now live in the best of circumstances, but you were designed and created to fulfill a purpose. I don't care what you say or what you have been told, Psalm 33:15 tells us that God "fashioned" us (NKJV).

Yep, you are God's fashion statement!

God would not create you for a purpose and then not help you achieve that purpose.

Consider this: In that very moment you were conceived, God was already pursuing you to bring you toward His purpose in creating you. In the union of your parents, God was about some serious Kingdom business. He had work that needed to be done in His Kingdom and He was creating a "servant son or daughter" to accomplish that for Him! Are you about the business He has called you to do for Him? The Word of God says that we are all called "according to His purpose" (2 Tim.1:9 KJV; see also 1 Pet. 2:21). (Better yet, do a word study on the word *purpose* in the Scriptures, if you don't think you have a purpose.)

In a moment we will see just what God thinks about us. Remember, no one knows us as well as the One who made us, and no one else's opinion carries any weight but His.

3. SATAN CAUSES US TO SEEK OTHER IDENTITIES.

This method of stealing identities is one that is multifaceted. Our creation of and the seeking of other identities has caused us to lose touch with our own true identity in Christ. Sometimes in the pursuit of other identities, the identity of who we truly are or should be is lost.

The most obvious of all are the denominational differences that have entered the Church. Remember, denominations are man's ideas, not Christ's. In First Corinthians 1:13, Paul asks the question, "Is Christ divided?" The obvious answer that Paul is looking for in that question is "No!" Yet sometimes our pursuit of our denominational identity causes us to be more identified with the denomination itself than with Christ. I so often have heard people say to me things like, "I try to be a good Catholic," or "My grandmother was a Baptist, my mother was a Baptist, and I am a Baptist." I asked one person if he knew the Lord, and he replied, "I am a Presbyterian!" "That's great," I said, "but do you know Jesus?"

I recall being at a luncheon during one of my speaking engagements, and the conversation turned to all the wonderful things that were happening in the Church around the world. My son Ben was with me and we both quickly noticed how one woman, speaking with a competitive tone, constantly mentioned what the Methodist church was doing or what program they were developing. Now, we know that the Methodist church is involved in good things and is part of the wonderful work being accomplished in the Church, but we quickly realized that her identity and how she felt about herself was wrapped up in being a Methodist and not as a child of God. She portrayed every other denomination as second-rate, and in that attitude God's purpose for her life was being undermined. Her identity as a joint heir with Christ was stolen by her focus on her identity as a Methodist, which is not what that denomination teaches!

In much the same way, titles such as Democrat or Republican and liberal or conservative cause us to draw our identities from our political persuasions. Becoming involved or listening to hot debates between these parties is very popular today and can distract us from what we are truly about. We begin to identify more with our party affiliation rather than our Christian heritage. There are professing Christians and even church leadership who allow their affiliation with a political party to persuade them to endorse or vote for a candidate who promotes viewpoints and principles that are contrary to Scripture. We need to remember to whom we belong and whose opinions and principles we endorse. We are Christians first and must endorse only those principles of political parties that line up with Scripture. We should never express opinions or beliefs that are contrary to God's.

I am often asked for my opinion or view on a controversial subject, to which I often reply, "I have no opinion on that subject." It usually evokes surprise and laughter, and I am told, "Everyone today has an opinion on that issue." My next reply is, "I have no opinion on this issue; because if the Word of God is already clear on a subject, who am I to have an opinion that is different from God's? I must accept His!" I don't have the right to have an opinion.

But you see...so many of us who name His name do not identify with His principles; thereby, we lose our identity. Jesus says in John chapter 17 that we are "in the world," but that we are not "of the world." Like I said before, we need to *infect* the world so that we can *affect* the world. We must inject our character into the world and not allow the world's character to infiltrate us, because it will steal our identity as citizens of Heaven.

Even cultural and ethnic identities steal our God-given identities and cause divisions within the Church. Listen! In Heaven, there will be no white churches, black churches, Asian churches, Spanish churches, or any other type of ethnic or culturally segregated churches. You see, in the mind of Christ, there is only one Church, *His Church*, and we all are part of His family. Fortunately, there is a growing trend in the Church today of multicultural and ethnic congregations (just like Heaven). My family is part of such a church, and what a blessing our cultural diversity is to us! I believe that the Holy Spirit is breaking down these walls within the Church and beginning to unite His family by the commonality of the blood that redeems us, the blood of Jesus Christ. In the Church we are truly "blood brothers" and "blood sisters," and there is truly no stronger bond or identity than that.

Our identity can also be stolen by our pursuit of another identity within the church. So many people want to be thought of as important in the church, so they seek out a position or a title, even stepping on others in order to get there. If they do not get what they want, they may sow discord within the church because they were passed over. These folks are more concerned with gaining the approval and recognition from others than developing their identity and true purpose and destiny in Christ. Why do we need a title to feel important in a church, when the Founder Himself died just for us...how important is that? I encounter people, and even pastors in the church, from time to time who are really engrossed with their position within the church. I have also been to churches where it seems everyone has a title and they introduce themselves as such. They will even go out of their way to let me know that they have a title or what they have accomplished.

Plain and simple, this is pride!

According to the Scriptures and to Jesus Himself, the most important title we can have as a believer is "servant." "Sitting down, He called the twelve and said to them, 'If anyone wants to be first, he shall be last of all and servant of all' " (Mark 9:35 NASU).

Do not misunderstand me. There is nothing wrong with being proud of your heritage or your political and ministerial associations or positions, except when they interfere with your primary role as "servant son and daughter," "salt and light," and "children of the light."

The truth is often hidden from us by those things that are artificial and secondary. Sometimes we cannot see the wheat of our lives for the tares sown therein! The expectations put on us by society to gain recognition and to acquire things is part of an artificially created environment or culture, one which was created for our failure. The whole humanistic philosophy, which teaches that we can become or do anything, is a half-truth and leaves out one very important ingredient...God! Jesus Christ's sacrifice on Calvary opens the door of our lives to return to God's original created intention for our lives. We need to walk through that door, step into the vision that God has for us, and grasp hold of the abundant life that Christ promised us. Colossians 1:12 tells us that those who have accepted the sacrifice of the Lord Jesus and made Him Lord of their lives (known as saints) have been qualified or enabled by God to share in the inheritance of all of what God intended for the "saints in the kingdom of light."

You see, by accepting Jesus as Lord and Savior of our lives, we have been delivered by God from the power of darkness, and He has conveyed us into the Kingdom of His Son. And...get this..."qualified" us to share in all the Kingdom's treasures!

Yes, we are talking about you here!

The enemy is so determined to keep you from finding out who you are that he does everything he can to steal your identity, because to steal your identity steals your power. Once you find out who you are and you get a vision for it, the devil's kingdom is threatened! (He stole that too!) The Bible tells us that satan is a "prince." Actually, I like to say that satan is a "king wanna be." He has lost track of one important fact though. He doesn't realize that there is a Prince ahead of him and that Jesus has already been crowned King. Satan was unsuccessful in deposing his rival prince at Calvary. As a result of the victory, God has crowned Jesus as King, and the rival prince is about to be driven out of the land!

Well, here is another tidbit from the "Holy Spirit Intelligence Report" (the Bible)—do you know what Ephesians 3:10 tells us? (Get ready...I love this!)

Simply put, it tells us (the Church) that we were made to teach the devil a lesson!

To the intent that now unto the principalities and powers in heavenly places might be known by the church the manifold wisdom of God (KJV).

Note that the "principalities and powers in heavenly places" refers to satan and his demons.

Jesus tells us in Matthew 11:12 that the Kingdom of Heaven has been forcefully advancing since the days of John the Baptist and that "forceful men lay hold of it."

My paraphrase of "forceful men lay hold of it" is…"purpose and Spirit-filled Christians kicking devil butt!"

The Church needs to be forceful (faithful) and courageous (disciplined and obedient) as we take steps to bring about Christ's Kingdom. *Let us rise up together and move against the gates of hell and act like those who have been destined to teach the devil a lesson!*

Let's peer into the mirror of God's Word. I want you to see exactly who He thinks you are and how He sees you. God's Word tells us how He views those who have received "so great salvation" (Heb. 2:3 KJV). This is not meant to be an exhaustive list, but I think you will get the idea.

God says we are:

1. *"A new creature"* (or creation). Old things have passed away (2 Cor. 5:17 KJV).

2. *"Ambassadors for Christ."* We are given authority to represent Him (2 Cor. 5:20 KJV).

3. *"The righteousness of God."* Because Christ covers our unrighteousness (2 Cor:5:21 KJV).

4. *"Saints of God."* Numerous scriptural references refer to us as "saints," which means "one set apart as God's possession." You belong to God and you will "judge the world" (1 Cor. 6:2).

5. *"More than conquerors."* Pretty powerful words, don't you think? (Rom. 8:37).

6. *"Children of God."* Who's your Daddy? (John 1:12, Phil. 2:15).

7. *"Holy and blameless."* Because we have accepted Christ's sacrifice and made Him Lord of our life (Eph. 1:4).

8. *"Bride."* Is there anyone more important to the groom at the wedding feast of the Lamb than the Bride? (Rev. 21:2).

9. *"Joint-heirs with Christ."* There are numerous places we are referred to as "heirs." We get what Christ gets from the father! (Rom. 8:17 KJV).

10. *"Partakers of the promise."* You're invited to the big party! (Eph. 3:6 KJV).

11. *"God's workmanship."* Remember, God don't make no junk! (Eph. 2:10). You're His fashion statement! (Psalm 33:15 KJV).

12. *"Citizens of Heaven."* Is there any greater citizenship? We are citizens with all the rights and privileges therewith! (Phil. 3:20).

13. *"Ones who will do greater works."* Jesus said this about us! (John 14:12).

14. *"Body of Christ."* It also says we are "members in particular." We have an individual purpose in a glorious body (Rom. 12:5).

15. *"Fellow workers and ministers of God."* We have a monumental task to accomplish in a sliver of time (2 Cor. 6:1-4).

16. *"Salt and light."* Salt gives things flavor and light illuminates and shows the way. We are the salt of the earth and the light of the revelation of Christ to the world (Matt. 5:13-14).

17. *"Children of the light."* Have you let the enemy steal your batteries? (Eph. 5:8).

18. *"Shining stars."* Have you always wanted to be a "star"? Forget American Idol! (Phil. 2:15).

19. *"Temple of the Holy Spirit."* Because the Spirit of God is in you, when others encounter you, they also encounter the Spirit of the living God! (1 Cor. 3:16).

20. *"Apple of His eye."* God says that any who mess with us are messing with the apple of His eye. You don't mess with God's kids or you will have Him to deal with! So when the devil messes with you...tell your Daddy! (Zech. 2:8).

21. *"Chosen generation."* The Greek word here means "favorite," and it means "elect." God voted for you! He picked you out special! (1 Pet. 2:9 KJV).

22. *"Royal priesthood."* I love this one! We are royalty because we are members of the King's family. That makes us princes and princesses! Just call me...Prince Buck! In our house lives Prince Buck and Princess Andrea! (Try it with your name.) Not only "royal," but also a "priest" in a fraternal order of priests. This is really exciting because according to Fausset's Bible Dictionary, there are four characteristics of the priest. He was (1) chosen of God; (2) the property of God; (3) holy to God; (4) *he offered gifts to God, and took back gifts from God* (Fausset's Bible Dictionary, Electronic Database Copyright (c)1998 by Biblesoft). How neat is that? Go ahead, talk amongst yourselves! (1 Pet. 2:9 KJV).

23. *"God's household."* You are an important part of God's family; you live in His house. You are family! *Family* literally means "father's house" (Eph. 2:19).

24. *"Those made alive with Christ."* Just as God raised Christ from the dead, He also raised us together with Christ to a new life (Eph. 2:5).

25. *"Those for whom Christ died."* Is there any greater than this? *You were worth dying for!* Jesus said that there is no greater love than a man lay down His life for His friends...then He went and did it! The fact is, if you were the only sinner in this world, He would have died just for you (Rom. 5:8).

Now you see why the devil wants to stop you—he sees your potential! You are a threat to all he has planned!

When we come to Jesus Christ and ask Him to be Lord of our life, God "anoints us" and "sets His seal of ownership on us" and He gives us the Holy Spirit as a "deposit" on His promises, guaranteeing them in our lives. We need to collect on this guarantee and pursue the promises of God in our life. I am talking about Second Corinthians 1:20-22 here. Listen to what the Word of God says about us…

For no matter how many promises God has made, they are "Yes" in Christ.

And so through Him the "Amen" is spoken by us to the glory of God.

Now it is God who makes both us and you stand firm in Christ. **He anointed us, set His seal of ownership on us, and put His Spirit in our hearts as a deposit, guaranteeing what is to come.**

The mind is where this battle of identity theft takes place; therefore, we need to take back the territory of our mind that satan has stolen so that we can truly know who we are.

We need a strategy, but where can we get it? Where else should we get it but from the Word of God. Oh how we need to focus on acquiring a deeper understanding of His Word! So many of God's people are spiritual illiterates, and satan uses this disadvantage to lead us astray. We all look for that silver bullet, the easy fix, but frankly, it takes work. When armies go into battle, they just don't drive into the territory on their tanks waving their flags; they have to fight! It's not fun; it takes work and commitment.

In winning the battle of Operation Mind Identity, we need to learn and apply what I call the "Three R's of the Mind." Let's take a look at them.

RENEW YOUR MIND

And be not conformed to this world: but be ye transformed by the renewing of your mind, that ye may prove what is that good, and acceptable, and perfect, will of God (Romans 12:2 KJV).

"Conversion," "coming to Christ," "accepting the Lord," or however you may refer to that moment when you called on Christ to be Lord of your life was only the beginning of the change that was to occur in your life. On that great day, your sin was blotted out, and you were declared righteous in God's sight because of the sacrifice of His Son, Jesus; you became part of God's great family. You received the indwelling of the Holy Spirit on that day, and now you need to know how to tap into that power within. Second Corinthians 5:17 says that on that day we became a "new creation," and Romans 12:1 says that we are to present that new creation to God as a "living sacrifice" as an "act of worship." Then verse 2 tells us not to be "conformed any longer to the pattern of this world." In the original Greek text, this word means to not "fashion ourselves according to the pattern of this world." Remember, you are God's "fashion statement." And as God's fashion statement, you should not be dressing yourself in the world's ideas about you. You need to start dressing yourself differently in your mind.

Listen to me! When you understand how God thinks about you, you begin to think differently. Thinking differently about yourself and who you are is what "transforms" you into that "new creation" God is talking about. You need to "renew your mind" by training or refashioning it to think about yourself as God thinks about you. Then you will be able to "test and approve," as the New International Version says, what God's perfect will is in your life, what His purpose is for your life.

You see, the mind is the ruling part of us; so in order to renew the whole person, we need to renew our mind. Is it any wonder that the enemy attacks us in our mind and tries to make us think that we are something we are not? When we become new, we act with new principles, new rules, and have a new design or creation. This transforming action is like taking on a new shape or figure. We receive a total makeover in the Spirit! Just like when we receive a physical makeover, we must submit to the designer so that we can be changed. We must also *discipline* (ah, there's that word again!) ourselves to begin to think like God thinks about us. When we come to Christ, there is a definite change that takes place in our lives, not only in our behavior and in our principles, but also in the way we think. The apostle Paul wrote to the Ephesians regarding this new creation idea and said, "In reference to your former manner of life, you lay aside the old self, which is being corrupted in accordance with the lusts of deceit, and that you *be renewed in the spirit of your mind, and put on the new self, which in the likeness of God* has been created in righteousness and holiness of the truth" (Eph. 4:22-24 NASU, emphasis added).

Did you catch that? We have been recreated in the "likeness of God." The "spirit of your mind" might be better translated to "attitude." Our attitude is the "spirit of our mind." *Our mind will follow our attitude!* If we have a negative attitude toward ourselves, the mind will wholeheartedly agree. Conversely, if we have a positive attitude, one based on the Word of God, our mind will wholeheartedly agree likewise. *Paul is actually saying that we need to renew our attitude and way of thinking about ourselves.* You can change a lot about yourself by changing your attitude. In fact, it is the first thing that has to happen before change can occur. This applies in every area of our life, but especially when it comes to our spiritual lives. We need to stop the "stinkin' thinkin' " as one of my coaches used to say. Do not focus on negative feelings; stop blaming others or circumstances, but focus on what God thinks of you, and take on that viewpoint of yourself.

RESET YOUR MIND

> *Those who live according to the sinful nature have their minds set on what that nature desires; but those who live in accordance with the Spirit have their minds set on what the Spirit desires. The mind of sinful man is death, but the mind controlled by the Spirit is life and peace* (Romans 8:5-6).

Hmm…"*…the mind controlled by the Spirit is life and peace.*" Isn't that what we all are seeking? Life and peace? Therefore, we need to change the settings in our mind. We need to reset our mind so it takes its direction and orders from the Spirit and not from the carnal mind that ruled our mortal bodies (and may still for many of us) before we made Jesus Lord of our lives. Remember, the mind is the ruling part of our bodies. Many of us forget, or were never taught, that at the moment of salvation, we needed to change the settings of our mind. While our soul is saved, our minds still may not yet be reset, no matter how long ago that day of salvation was for you.

Okay, Okay, I know, it is easier said than done. So how do we reset our mind?

First, we need to learn and repeat all the things that God says we are. Memorize that list in this chapter until you "put it in your mind" as one of my college professors used to say. These things are from the Word of God; believe it and do not doubt. Do not go back to those old lies of the past. When the devil tries to reconvince you of those lies, declare, "I am a saint, a child of God, one of the King's kids, indwelt by the Holy Spirit!" Then quote Jesus: "Get thee behind me, satan" (Luke 4:8 KJV).

Second, we need to avoid the trap of blaming someone else. We need to own up to our own mistakes and bad attitudes, and establish a new direction in our mind. It is not our parent's fault, our race, where we were born, or the lack of opportunity we have had. I will never forget the conversation I had with a man who was born in Africa, lived in nothing, so poor it was worse than poverty, was orphaned, and nearly killed many times by the Muslim government because he was a Christian. He eventually came to the United States, arrived with nothing, got an education and a good job, and was accumulating wealth. He admitted to me that he did not understand how so many people in the United States never seemed to rise above a certain level, considering all the opportunity that was here. You see, he had a renewed and reset mind and an attitude based on who he was in Christ. He also had numerous things going against him, but the one thing that overrode them all...*he had the mind of Christ.*

Third, we need to visualize. Visualization is very popular today, and it has spiritual applications. Visualize what is not present reality (I am out of debt, I am successful), as though it were. As Romans 4:17b says, "Call those things which be not as though they were" (KJV).

We need to make a decision to overcome in Christ—"set our face like flint" (Isa. 50:7) to see and think of ourselves as God does and grab hold of that purpose and destiny He has planned for us. We have got to get our "game face on" with the devil and have an attitude of victory, not hang our head in defeat!

When I played football, I did well and was moved up with the older guys because of my ability. I remember when I went out on the field for the first time and was very aware that the other guys were older, stronger, and more experienced than me. While waiting for the play to begin, the team captain suddenly said, "Man, you look like you are going to wet your pants! You've got to get your game face on. *Don't let them see your fear!* Hey, I've seen you play, and they're the ones who should be afraid."

I learned a lesson that day that I have used throughout my life. Knowing how the team captain and my teammates thought about me gave me confidence and changed my attitude—and I "got my game face on." I was pumped! During the first tackle of the game, I hit the guy so hard I caused him to fumble the ball, which one of my teammates recovered. The fear disappeared. I learned that my attitude, and the thoughts of someone important and significant, could affect my success. Do you see the application?

Someone important thinks a lot about you and has great confidence in you and the abilities He has created in you. You need to reset your mind, change your attitude, and get up off the couch and do something. Hit that devil so hard with the Word, that he goes someplace else. The devil is the only one I ever tell to "go to hell." In his case, it is not profanity; it is simply a statement of fact! That's where he's headed and he doesn't like to be reminded. You have got to get your game face on—keep it on and do something!

Like I always say, "If you want to run with the big dogs, you can't sit on the porch!"

RESURRECT YOUR MIND

And hath raised us up together, and made us sit together in heavenly places in Christ Jesus (Ephesians 2:6 KJV).

We need to have a resurrection mind, one that knows Jesus has been raised from the dead in victory over persecution, victory over the flesh, victory over sin, raised to a new life, that abundant life that Jesus promised to those who call upon His name.

We need to think like that!

On the day we accepted Christ, we passed from death into life, and according to Scripture, one day we will be raised to life incorruptible to live eternally with Christ (see 1 Cor.15:42). We must get a vision of that life; and just as our decision to serve Christ spiritually resurrected us with Christ, we have to bring our minds into that resurrection power as well. How do we have a resurrected mind? We receive that as the prize when through faith and knowledge of the Scriptures, we learn exactly who we are in Christ. We stop believing the lies sown by the enemy into our lives, and we *renew* and *reset* our minds. Our minds, once renewed and reset, will resurrect our lives here on earth to a new life in Christ.

Many have come to Christ, only to have never achieved their own purpose and high calling God has planned for them, because they have never renewed and reset their mind in order to resurrect it to the abundant life in Christ. Our goal is to achieve the resurrected mind that the Bible refers to as the "mind of Christ." The Word of God says that we can understand what the Lord is thinking, which would include what He thinks about us!

"Who can know what the Lord is thinking? Who can give Him counsel? But we can understand these things, for we have the mind of Christ" (1 Cor 2:16 NLT).

Spiritual matters are foolishness to the world, because they have not come to faith in Jesus Christ—they have never received the Holy Spirit. They have, therefore, not been able to renew, reset, and resurrect their minds. Hence, many do not understand spiritual issues or understand us "born-againers"! (Remember, Jesus is the one who coined that term—see John chapter 3.)

Before we go on with any further discussion regarding the coming financial revolution of the Church, I feel I should address some of our readers who may not understand their salvation or may not even be sure that they qualify for the promises found in the Word to God's children. They are not sure that they have become a member of God's family through faith in Jesus Christ. What do I mean by that? I mean that the Word of God teaches that we all are sinners and we need a Savior. Only those who receive the free gift of Jesus' redemption for their sins and accept Him as Lord of their life are the ones who become heir to all the promises in the Word of God.

In the next chapter, we will discuss the plan of salvation God has for us and how we can know we are part of God's family. We will also discuss satan's strategy to undermine God's calling in our lives. If you are not sure you qualify for the promises in the Word of God, please read on. The next chapter will help you to better understand your need for a Savior, why the world is the way it is, and how you can become part of God's family and an heir to all that He has promised.

CHAPTER 18

STRATEGY OF SATAN AND GOD'S PLAN

There was a time when a war raged in the heavens. Michael the archangel and the forces of God fought against lucifer (satan), a powerful and former archangel called "son of the morning," and his followers. Lucifer had been created with the free moral choice to compliment God's desire to love and be loved. Just as God wanted man to exhibit his love for Him by subordination and obedience as the created being, lucifer was to hold his position in the heavens out of love.

But lucifer began to "rationalize," and rationalization will lead to sin. He began to think about the restrictions placed on him. "What is God holding back? God loves me...or does He? What is He trying to hide? Perhaps I can be like God and this is how He controls me." Once this questioning begins, then covetousness sets in: "I can be like Him!" The desire to obey is replaced by covetousness, which is then overtaken by pride: "How dare He hold me back!" Pride leads to action and in lucifer's case, disobedience and sin.

Lucifer sought to discredit God and convinced others to rally behind him in his quest to "be like God"—to steal His identity. Other heavenly beings under lucifer's leadership (angels) were tempted and joined him. The battle then began between those loyal to God and those who were disobedient. Evil entered the heavens because of this disobedience; consequently, lucifer and his host, one third of the angels (demons), were cast out of Heaven by the archangel Michael and the forces of God.

Lucifer lost the first battle.

Did God then create evil? Not at all! God created the ability to choose. Why did God do this? God claims to be omniscient (all-knowing) by His nature. If this is true, then did He not know that this would happen? The answer: Of course, He did!

You see, although God is by nature omniscient, He is also a loving being. A loving being is one who wants to be loved as well as one who loves. Although God created beings that would choose disobedience, He would also create real reciprocal love in the universe. The person we love is someone who has given us something we need in our life, someone to which we have a love commitment. We choose to love people, and they choose to love us. And in order to love, we must take chances. Sometimes we love in spite of problems and shortcomings on the part of the other person, and sometimes we can be hurt. God in His creation of love also created a deeper love, an unconditional love, the kind of love that sought to redeem a fallen mankind.

Lucifer continued his attack on earth upon God because God *loved* mankind and man was continuing to obey God. Lucifer determined that he must discredit God, for as long as unquestioning obedience was given to God by His creation, lucifer would never be able to attain the status of God. Lucifer, urged on by pride, (which is never rational) contended that he could win, and headed for the Garden of Eden to confront Eve and her husband, Adam.

Interestingly, lucifer, the king of liars, did not tell Eve an obvious lie; instead, he told her a half-truth (which is still a lie!)—eating of the tree of good and evil would open Adam and Eve's eyes. The truth part was that it would open their eyes to all that disobedience would bring into one's life—evil, death, and eternal separation from their loving God. Eve would have never known the travail of childbirth or the loss of a child through murder. Adam would have never known how hard labor felt or how it feels to grow old, get sick, and face death. Lucifer did lie because he did not tell the whole truth!

In telling a half-truth to Adam and Eve, he convinced them to use their ability to rationalize, which brought on a covetous spirit. When pride came into bloom, the "I can be great, I can know all that God knows" attitude caused Adam and Eve to disobey. Lucifer had succeeded! He had discredited God in Adam and Eve's eyes so that they were willing to disobey what God had asked of them to prove their love. Their blood, now polluted with the knowledge of evil and disobedience, would continue to pollute all men for all generations. If Adam and Eve had refused, lucifer would have fled, forever defeated. However, they did not, and death passed to all men.

Lucifer had won the second battle and had succeeded in destroying all mankind...or so he thought.

God's unconditional love for man, in spite of what he had done, caused God to prepare a way for man to atone for his sin. There were people such as Abraham who had a desire to love and serve God, but they still had a polluted bloodstream. King David, in spite of his love for God, had a sinful nature. Although these men loved God and were obedient, neither of them could ever stand in the presence of the Almighty God without atonement being made for their sinful nature. They would never be good enough within themselves to enter Heaven.

Lucifer was not by any means through. He knew of God's ability to love unconditionally. He also saw that in spite of his perceived success, some men still chose to be obedient to God, so he decided that he must somehow continue to discredit God in order to keep man beaten down. (Remember, lucifer's covetous spirit and his pride continues to make him irrational. He thinks he can rule in God's place. He views God's ability to love unconditionally as a weakness!) He felt he could be successful as he held man hostage in a world where evil and disobedience abound and where man's sinful nature separates him eternally from God. Lucifer believed that he had stolen God's creation from God!

However, God launched a plan to atone for man. The penalty of death and separation from God would be paid once and for all.

God-loving and God-serving men and women die, but they die in their own sin and still must face eternal separation from God, for good and evil cannot abide together. You see...death holds men in its grasp because of their sin. A person's own sin is what keeps the lock on the outside of the doors of hell, which will hold fallen man there forever...unless there is a way of redemption!

In God's plan, a sinless man would have to pay a sin price; sin's power would not be able to hold this person in death because he would have no personal sin. He would break the bars of hell and therefore escape. His spotless death would pay the price for others' sin, because He had none of his own. God Himself would have to father this man, for He was the only sinless being in the universe that could do so.

Lucifer's work was cut out for him as God sent a sinless man into the world through the virgin birth. God's sinless spiritual "genes" or nature would be combined with Mary's sinful human genes or nature to create the God-Man, Jesus. Biology tells us that genes from a man and a woman combine to form a new person. But how could God's "perfect" or "good" genes combine with Mary's "sinful" or "evil" genes to form a sinless man? If anything, it would seem that Jesus would have less of a sin nature than other men, half as sinful. This question has led some to conclude that Mary must have been sinless too. This is not possible, however, because in order for her to be sinless, both of her parents would have had to be sinless. And we know that all men since Adam have been born with a sin-polluted bloodstream.

In the spiritual, good always wins over evil. The two are incompatible with each other and cannot coexist in the same place. At conception, Mary's egg was fertilized spiritually by the Holy Spirit. The Holy Spirit's "sperm" fertilizing the egg was like light penetrating a dark room...and the darkness was dispersed! In the zygote, or the fertilized egg that became Jesus, imperfection was incompatible with perfection, and the imperfection was driven out. The "pollutants" in Mary's bloodstream put there by the sin of our original parents and passed on to her by her natural parents, was driven and kept out of that zygote by the presence of God's holy nature in the fertilization process as well as in the womb. Jesus was sinless!

Lucifer, again, had the same task put before him that he had met in the Garden of Eden. (Remember, lucifer is not omniscient and did not know Jesus was coming.) Lucifer pulled out all the tricks on this "Son of God," and I believe that Jesus was tempted and tried throughout His entire life, worse than any of us have or ever will be. Lucifer recognized Jesus and His sinless, obedient nature. He had never seen a man on the Earth like this man since Adam before his fall. A man with no sin! Imagine lucifer's fear! Disobedience was the key strategy against Jesus, as it was with Adam. "Get Jesus to disobey God" was Lucifer's cry to his henchmen (demons). "Attack not only Him but also those with whom He comes in contact."

Jesus, driven by His love for the Father and His desire to obey unconditionally, proved to be an insurmountable task for lucifer. He failed over and over in convincing Jesus to yield to temptation.

Those around Jesus were a different story however. So lucifer decided that if he could not get Jesus to disobey, his best effort was to get others to destroy Jesus. Lucifer, recognizing Jesus' physical side, believed that once Jesus was murdered, He would be held in the prison of death and out of the way.

Satan tempted those around Jesus to rise up against the Son of God, and so Jesus was crucified and died, and then descended into that prison of eternal separation from God. Within that prison, unforgiven or unatoned sin locked the gate that holds one there. And so, without redemption, the unrighteous person is separated for all eternity with no hope. Satan, however, failed to recognize that the lock on that prison was a man's own personal, unforgiven sin. Whereas, Jesus, being sinless, could not be locked in and so escaped, not only breaking the bars of that gate but also taking the key!

Jesus then went on to take that key to the Father to trade it for an eviction notice, which Jesus will serve on ole lucifer, when He returns to set up His Kingdom!

Get all excited about this! Imagine the look on satan's face!

God is a just God. He recognized that a sin price was paid by the One who had no sin—Jesus. Death is only for the sinful. Hell is for the unforgiven sinner! God recognized that Jesus had suffered unfairly and declared that the price for *all* disobedience had been paid and that the ability for man to choose had once again been restored. God declared that all who would accept and claim this canceling out or atonement of this sin debt and who would choose to be obedient to God, would be able to break through the bars of this death prison using the key that Jesus provided! They would be brought into the presence of the Almighty God by the sinless One who had unjustly paid the sin price. God would allow Jesus to redeem those who, even though not perfect, chose obedience to God in their lives here on Earth.

Whereas, those who would continue to choose disobedience would remain in that death prison (hell) to ultimately, upon leaving this world, reside with the one they chose to be obedient to—the original sinner himself! Lucifer, whom we now call satan, would also be trapped in this prison, locked in by his own sin.

In which category do you fall? If you have not chosen to receive Jesus as Lord of your life, there is hope for you. Just read on!

If God is omniscient, He must have known that things would go as they did. He must have known that lucifer would disobey and rebel and that man would also sin and be destroyed by that sin. Why then did He ever create lucifer and Adam? Why did he put Adam in the same place where lucifer had been cast down, in a garden where lucifer had sown tares?

Why did God create all this grief for Himself?

God, as we learned, is a loving God and He desires to be surrounded by those who *choose* to love Him. A loving being with no one to love or to receive love in return is the loneliest of all. God at the end of this earthly saga of sin, disobedience, and death will be surrounded by those He loves. He will be surrounded by those people who, of their own free will and volition, have shown in this earthly life that they have chosen to be obedient to Him under earthly circumstances and love Him. No eternal test will need to be administered to those of us who join Him. Our love through the ultimate test of obedience will have already been proven to God. No tree of the knowledge of good and evil will be planted in Heaven. We will be with God in a sinless, loving paradise. There will be no one to sow tares in that Kingdom; he will be under lock and key for all eternity. He will have been cast into hell, the place God has prepared for him for all eternity. Unfortunately, there will be others there as well— those who chose to disobey and live their own lives their own way.

You see…God, when He thought of creating lucifer and Adam, saw the whole picture. He saw all the chapters of man—past, present, and future. He saw the end result…and it was good—the loving family of God, together forever!

What will happen to those who choose not to receive Jesus Christ's gift of salvation and accept Him as Lord and Savior of their lives and live in obedience to God? The Bible says they will join satan in hell for all eternity. It is a place of torment and eternal separation from God, a place where satan is the only one who will have had no choice in going there. Hell was created for satan; all others will be there of their own free will, a free will they exercised while on earth when they chose not to serve and obey God.

Would a loving God condemn a person to hell for all eternity?

No, it is their own sin that condemns them. God has provided a way of escape—Jesus Christ! It is their own choice that they are condemned to hell. No choice is a default choice. You must make a conscious and heartfelt decision to follow Christ. It does not just happen! You are not a believer just because your parents were…God has no grandchildren, only children. You are not a believer just because you go to church, or have been baptized as an infant. You must make a conscious decision! I made mine in July 1964 at Camp Sankanac in Spring City, Pennsylvania, in the Mohicans cabin just after evening devotions. Where and when did you make yours? If you do not know, why don't you make that moment right now?

Once while talking about the gift of salvation to someone, the man replied to me, "I have tried to live a good life and do the right thing. I can truthfully say that when I get up and look in the mirror every day, I have no regrets. I have been benevolent and caring toward others and fair and honest in my dealings….You mean to tell me, that God would allow me to go to hell, and that how I have lived would not be good enough to get me into Heaven?"

We were sitting in his living room at the time, and I reached for a Bible and told him that I was not the best one to answer that question. I then related an event to him where Jesus was asked that same question by a man named Nicodemus, recorded in the Book of John. "Jesus answered and said unto him, Verily, verily, I say unto thee, Except a man be born again, he cannot see the kingdom of God" (John 3:3 KJV).

This Scripture is where we get the term "born again," and Jesus was the first to use it!

How about you? What choice have you made with your life? Who have you chosen to follow? Have you chosen Jesus and obedience out of your own free will, or have you chosen some other way? Remember, there really is no other way. Jesus said in John 14:6, "I am the way, the truth, and the life: no man cometh unto the Father, but by Me" (KJV).

No, it is not true that all religions lead to God; if they did, then Jesus is wrong and...I don't think so! If you do not think you have made a choice, remember the default choice is eternal separation from God and those you love.

If you are not part of God's family here on earth, you cannot be part of His family after this life. According to the Bible, there is no second chance after death. In addition, the promises of the Bible in the area of finances and in all other areas of our life are only for God's children.

If you are a reader who has never made a decision to make Jesus Christ Lord of your life, or if you are unsure you are part of God's family, would you make that decision now? You would be a welcome addition to the family of God, and we sure would love to have you with us forever in Christ's Kingdom. Being a member of God's family would entitle you to all that God has promised in this life and in the Kingdom life to come. Let me review these important points with you that will lead you to make a decision for Christ and qualify you as a child of God and all the other things we talked about in the last chapter. I have included ample Scripture references to substantiate these points.

The Bible tells us:

1. *All men are sinners.* (See Romans 3:10, 3:23; Isaiah 64:6; Jeremiah 17:9; James 2:10.)

2. *The penalty of sin is death.* (See Romans 6:23; Ezekiel 18:20.)

3. *You must be perfect and sinless to enter Heaven.* (See Revelation 21:27; Habakkuk 1:13; Psalm 5:4.)

4. *You cannot do anything on your own to obtain perfection.* (See Ephesians 2:8-9, Galatians 2:16, Romans 4:5.)

5. *God provided a perfect sin-bearer (Jesus) and imputes to us His righteousness.* (See Second Corinthians 5:21; Philippians 3:9; Isaiah 53:6; First Peter 3:18.)

6. *We need only to believe in the Lord Jesus Christ as our personal Savior and there is salvation in no other.* (See John 3:16; Romans 10:9; John 1:12; Acts 16:31.)

7. *You can be certain of your salvation now and know that your salvation cannot be lost because eternal life is eternal.* (See John 6:37,39; First John 5:13; John 10:28; Hebrews 10:10,14; First Peter 1:5).

It does not matter what your past has been or what you have done. God is a God of restoration, and His grace is sufficient to save you and turn your life around. Just as no one is good enough to get into Heaven on their own merit, no one is bad enough not to receive so great a salvation as Jesus provided.

I don't care (more importantly, God doesn't care) whether you are Catholic, Baptist, Methodist, Presbyterian, Lutheran, Charismatic, Pentecostal, or another faith or background, or what your Mamma or Daddy was...

God and I just want to know...do you know Jesus?

I don't mean, know about Him or what He has done; but do you have a personal relationship with Him? Answering this question is the most important thing you can ever do in this *temporary* life because it determines where you will spend eternity. There is no second chance after this life. Eternity is a long time, so you better make your reservations with Christ in Heaven. Remember, the default decision is to spend eternity according to the plans God has for satan—eternal separation from God and from all others. Remember, your body dies, but your soul or spirit does not. All you must do is accept the free gift of eternal life provided by God through Jesus Christ. So let me ask you again...do you know Jesus?

Answer this question now before you read further because the Bible tells us that the time of Jesus' coming again will come upon us as a "thief in the night." The world will be caught by surprise—will you?

But of the times and the seasons, brethren, ye have no need that I write unto you. For yourselves know perfectly that the day of the Lord so cometh as a thief in the night. For when they shall say, Peace and safety; then sudden destruction cometh upon them, as travail upon a woman with child; and they shall not escape (1 Thessalonians 5:1-3 KJV).

What is your answer?

If you would like to be part of God's family—or maybe you are not sure you have ever asked Jesus to be Lord of your life, leading you to abundant life—would you pray the following prayer with those of us in God's family who already have:

Lord Jesus, I acknowledge that I am a sinner and that I need a Savior to be seen as righteous in God's eyes. I believe You died on the cross for me and that Your sacrifice has covered my sins. I ask You to come into my life and save me and to be Lord of my life. Change me, Lord, and lead me into the abundant life that You have promised. Thank You, Lord, for saving me. In Your precious name, I pray. Amen.

If you have prayed that prayer, let me welcome you to the family of God and to eternal life in Jesus Christ!

Maybe some of you have made a decision for Christ in the past but are not living for Him today. Why don't you now take this opportunity to recommit yourself to Him and begin to walk in obedience to His will? If you would like to recommit yourself, take a moment and ask His forgiveness and renew that commitment to Him. Begin to walk in obedience to the One who loves you with an everlasting love. Pray your own prayer or you can pray the following prayer if you need help.

Lord Jesus, I am sorry that I have been disobedient and have strayed from You. Forgive me for my unfaithfulness. I thank You for Your faithfulness to love me in spite of my sins. Create in me a clean heart, Lord, and renew a right spirit in me. I recommit myself to You and ask that You help me to walk in obedience to Your will in my life. Thank You, Lord. In Your precious name, I pray. Amen.

Now, let me encourage you to find a gospel-preaching and Bible-teaching church to become part of, where you can be encouraged and taught so that you can grow further in your walk with Jesus Christ.

If you have accepted Jesus Christ while reading this book, or if you have recommitted your life to Christ, I urge you to let us know by completing the page in the back of this book and sending it to us at the address on the form. We have something we would like to send you to help you in your new walk with Christ.

The Lord told me that a number of my readers who would be looking for financial help would not be part of the family of God. It is my prayer that all readers from this point on in the book would now be considered "family." By the way, *family* means "Father's house"! If I never get to meet you in this life...I will see you at Father's house!

CHAPTER 19

TIMOTHY! GUARD WHAT HAS BEEN ENTRUSTED TO YOU

Paul's exhortation to Timothy causes us to ponder what the pastor's role and the role of other church leaders should be in the area of finances. I don't mean to "let the proverbial cat out of the bag" here, but many of you pastors and leaders are in the same boat as are many of the people in your pastoral charge. Many of you are suffering the same condemnation that they are, and you are afraid someone will find out. How do I know? I have been an advisor in the Christian community for nearly 30 years. Need I say more? On numerous occasions a pastor has admitted to me that he did not readily accept a financial ministry's help because he himself did not want to take a look at his own finances, let alone bring up the subject to the entire church! Many pastors suffer from financial difficulties simply because their congregation is in bondage and consequently cannot pay an adequate salary to the pastor.

I have found that pastors and leaders have resisted the assistance of a financial ministry for a number of reasons. Here are some for you to consider:

1. They feel threatened by allowing another minister or ministry to teach a subject in their church that they themselves feel unequipped to handle.

2. They believe that the ministry or minister just wants to sell something (either services or materials) and is using the approach as a way to increase business.

3. They themselves have an unresolved issue in their lives in the area of finances.

4. They are afraid to address such a taboo topic because of the negative feedback they might receive.

5. They have no understanding of the depth of the financial problem in the Church at large and especially in their local church.

6. They are afraid that starting a financial ministry in their church will require too much of their already precious time.

Let me briefly comment on each of these reasons. Hopefully, I will address every concern in order to motivate pastors and leaders to establish an active financial ministry in their church or para-church organization.

REASON 1

Many pastors feel unequipped to handle a financial ministry and feel that it is a put-down to ask an outside ministry to assist. Let us call this attitude what it is—pride! Sometimes in life and in ministry, we need a specialist; and as leaders, we need to be transparent. The most successful pastor is usually a pastor who is very transparent. A poll conducted by Crown Financial Ministries revealed that 85 percent of all pastors feel unequipped to deal with financial issues, so you are not alone.

REASON 2

Often, church leaders believe that a financial minister or ministry has something to sell—either materials or services. Yes, I am the first to admit that there are a number of people, especially in the financial services field, who are looking for clients and prospecting for individuals through seminars at a church. However, this is not everyone's agenda. My advice is to ask the individual what it is they wish to present. Ask to see their outline. If they are presenting investments and offering information that might cause someone to seek their services in these areas, then it might be best to consider some alternatives. Seek out a ministry or minister with a record of accomplishment and one who can address the real problem in your church. That problem is the lack of knowledge of God's directives and the financial bondage that Christians are experiencing. This type of message is not going to make anyone any money! Ministering to the church in this manner has instead cost me a lot of money. I do it because of a calling—not due to personal gain.

I grow tired of leaders being so afraid of allowing the wrong person to come in, that nothing ever happens. Listen to me! Anyone presenting what the Bible has to say about finances, who preaches a message concerning debt reduction and learning how to manage God's money is not making a lot of money. Let me assure you, I conducted this type of ministry for years and never made any money; in fact, as I said, it cost me money. I have even been chided by unbelieving associates for being involved in this type of ministry because it is unproductive in developing a financial advisor's practice. They are right!

Let me tell you what you do get!

You get a lot of desperate Christians seeking your help with creditors and with debt management! Considering the investment of time, an advisor would be best to prospect somewhere else. In all the years I have practiced, I have learned where it is profitable to prospect, and unfortunately, the church is low on the list. However, my goal is to move it up! Over the years I have spent countless number of hours a month counseling Christians in this area and I consider it seeds planted for a financial revolution in the Church!

The Church can benefit from professional help in other ways too. I have had the experience of having someone contact me to follow up on an illustration he heard me give during a message or seminar. In one instance, I assisted a person in making an anonymous gift to his church—a retirement account that paid for all the new seating in the church they were building. How much did I make on that? Nothing! You must consider the heart and the motivation of an individual, and as always, references are important! Proverbs 16:2 tells us that God weighs the motives of a man.

Consider this: If an advisor provides a valuable service to a believer or a church, why should he not be paid? I have seen ministries so afraid to work with professional people that it borders on paranoia. We believe that God heals people, but sometimes He uses doctors in that process. We allow guest ministers to sell tapes or books to support their ministry after a service. Why should a financial advisor whose heart is right not assist a Christian or a church with a matter, and be compensated? In Second Corinthians 12:13-18, Paul indicates that he was criticized for the way he handled his business and his ministry. Paul was a tentmaker and the implication here is that he sold tents to believers! In First Thessalonians 2:4 he refers to the accusation that he had "tricked them" for personal gain. If someone is of God, your association with them will be blessed. If he is not, let God take care of it!

Let me make another observation here. I have had contact with many Christian advisors in the legal, accounting, medical, and financial fields over the years. I have heard it said too often in private conversation with these advisors something we all hate to admit. They are as I am—much saddened by the fact that all too often, Christians seek out Christian advisors in the hopes of receiving some free advice. The Bible says that a "workman is worthy of his hire" (see Matt. 10:9-10 KJV; Luke 10:7).

There are established ministries such as Crown Financial Ministries who have trained and screened people who can help you in these areas. These ministries sell their materials, but the sale of the materials only helps defray the cost of the development of these resource materials and support the ministry. The main support of the ministry comes from donations. Their goal is to help the Church build its own financial ministry—not take over.

Reason 3

I mentioned that I have had pastors admit to me that they were resistant to my ministry because they themselves had some unresolved issues regarding finances in their life. They also knew that opening up this type of ministry in their church would cause them to confront the same issues in their own life, so they chose the path to "ignore it, and it will go away!" (No, it won't.) In my experience, financial difficulties in the leadership's own life also creates difficulties in the finances of the church. How the home is run usually results in how the church is run. I am not talking only of pastors here but to church board members and eldership as well.

I remember being asked a number of years ago to come to a church board meeting to offer some guidance in the area of the church's finances. They were initially very concerned whether I would charge them for my advice or not. I told them that I would be happy to consult with them in the name of the Lord, and that I would let Him multiply the seed I was planting.

I arrived at the meeting, and as they presented the situation they were dealing with, I noticed one important fact—the pastor was not part of the meeting. I listened intently as they spoke. After I had gained a clear understanding of the church's situation and problems, it was time for me to speak.

I asked them if I could ask one question before I laid out my assessment of the finances and of what action should be taken. Given an affirmative answer, I noted that the pastor was not there and asked why as the spiritual leader of the church, he was not involved.

I guess they had hoped I would not notice, and after some interesting body language and some looking around at each other, the chairman replied, "Buck, you see, that is part of the problem. We did not invite him to this meeting because we believe that we have these problems because he does not emphasize giving and tithing enough. Consequently, we are struggling to keep this ministry operating out of the red. The people love him, and he is good in so many other areas, but we are considering asking him to leave. In fact, we have already put out feelers for his replacement. So you see, we thought it best if he were not here. He doesn't even know we are having this meeting."

I thought long and hard, but I could not for the life of me, remember any disappearing tricks. I thought about jumping up and yelling, "Hey, look over there!" and then running out the door when their heads were turned, but realized that was too juvenile, even for me. I did not like the work the Lord had called me to do this night, let me tell you! I had seen the church books and I had seen the enemy, and it wasn't the pastor! I looked at my sleeve and wished I had worn one of my older sport coats, for I was sure that what I was about to tell them would cause me to be tossed out the red front door of that church, with my briefcase tossed out after me.

I quietly prayed, the Lord confirmed, and so I began my assessment of the problem. When the offerings came in, they all were dumped into one account and all bills were paid as best they could be. There was no management, no budget, and no accountability! Actually, the receipts were adequate, but with poor money management and a lack of attention to budget, money was spent haphazardly.

I, in the kindest way I could, pointed out the problem, and then with astonishment I heard myself say, "I don't think the problem rests entirely with your pastor, gentlemen. I think the bulk of the responsibility rests right here in this room."

"And it was quiet in heaven for about a half hour" (see Rev. 8:1).

I could sense the angels looking on, wondering which one was going to be sent to escort me home to glory.

After some wiggling and shuffling of feet, one of the men said, "Well...you have given us some pretty convincing evidence here. I wish you were wrong, but it appears you are right. I guess we need to reconsider our ways and to make some changes."

Ah, saved by the Holy Spirit moving in the heart of an honest man!

Phew! I got away with that one! It is scary sometimes when the Holy Spirit uses your voice.

Then, I heard myself say another daring thing!

"I suggest you start by meeting with your pastor on this." I then offered some practical advice and suggested that they might want to hire a professional bookkeeper to help them get an adequate system established. They did so, and last I knew, the same pastor was still there and things had turned around.

I have seen this problem in varying degrees in the management of the finances of churches and ministries of all sizes. I want you to grasp this concept. *The management of the church is symptomatic of the financial conditions and biblical financial understanding of the individual leaders in the church.*

REASON 4

In a previous chapter, I addressed the fact that many people believe that discussing finances in the church is a taboo subject. This reveals that they do not know that finance is the second-most discussed subject in the Bible.

It hurts the most when you hit people in their pocketbooks, and especially when it comes from the pulpit, it elicits all kinds of responses. I remember one of my pastors telling me that he hated when the board asked him to speak on tithing. He would joke and say that he would break out in a rash. The reason was that he would get all kinds of comments, both good and bad, both approving and critical when he did.

Hey, what can I say here? The Master is coming back, and we are accountable! Leadership is also accountable for teaching this subject to God's people.

REASON 5

I am amazed at how Christians can keep their financial situations a secret from their brothers and sisters in the Lord and from their pastors. Many pastors have told me that they were not only surprised at how many, but also at who was experiencing difficulties in being financially faithful. There are people who appear affluent (previously referred to as "cash flow rich"). Everything is financed, and he or she is within a few months from bankruptcy, but all is well as long as the cash flow continues.

People will talk to the pastor about their family, their marriage, their job—all sorts of things—but money is the one thing people have the most difficulty sharing about. Why? Because they fear that one question: "Are you tithing?" The answer is, "No," and they fear the condemnation that will most certainly come, which frankly is already upon them and paralyzing them!

My experience is that 9 out of 10 couples I have counseled have never shared the problem with the pastor that they are sharing with me, and it usually relates to tithing.

When people come to me to request help, I always ask them where they worship. Usually after I receive a few requests from the same church, I then contact the pastor to try to convince him to set something up to help God's people with their finances. It has often been my experience that pastors will tell me that they do not think it is much of a problem at their church. I then ask, "Pastor, why do you think I contacted you?" He is usually surprised when he realizes that I know about personal circumstances in his church that he is unaware of.

REASON 6

Even with other obstacles out of the way, oftentimes a pastor or leader is concerned that a financial ministry will take up too much of his time, time that is already stretched to the limit. And so, they put it off, waiting for that free time that never seems to be available.

Just as the enemy, the devil, keeps us so busy that we cannot focus on getting our finances in order, so he will seek to keep the leadership's focus elsewhere as well!

My advice is that the pastor appoints a lay coordinator to oversee this ministry and develop it. The resource ministries will assist him in doing so, requiring very little of the pastor's time. The pastor needs to learn to delegate this responsibility. In time this delegation may actually free up more of his time as his flock is released from the bondage of debt and becomes free to serve in more areas of the church.

Yes, as I said in the beginning, this is the biggest problem in the church today. Why? Because no other problem affects the church in all areas as much as this one does.

So let us go back to the passage in First Timothy chapter 6 where Paul exhorts Pastor Timothy to guard what is entrusted to him, which immediately follows the instructions to "command" the people in his pastorate to be rich toward God (just like Jesus did in Luke 12:21), to be generous, and to lay up their treasures as "a firm foundation for the coming age."

Part of what Timothy was to guard was the wealth of his flock. The "wolves" wanted to sneak in and steal it! The pastor guards through the full teaching of the Word on the subject and by holding them accountable as stewards.

His flock is the "stewards," and the pastor is the "trustee."

The trustee is the one given charge of that which is put in trust. His job is to oversee, to instruct, and to see that the beneficiaries of the trust adhere to the tenets or instructions of the "trust." The trustee is charged with the responsibility to see to it that the wishes of the one who granted the trust are carried out. These wishes are recorded in what is known as the "trust document." In the event that the beneficiaries do not act in accordance with the trust, it is the trustee's responsibility to go to the authority, which is the court, and ask the court to enforce the directives of the trust.

Let us consider an example.

I am the beneficiary of an educational trust. The trustee releases funds to me from the trust to be used for my education. I receive the check, and let's just say I decide to use it for a vacation to the Bahamas.

The trustee discovers this and will contact me. He may ask me to return the money or scold me for not following the directives of the trust. However, the trustee has no authority to force me to do anything. The only thing he can do is take me to the authority, again in this case, the court system, which would enforce the directives of the trust document, declare me in violation of the trust agreement, and take corrective action against me.

With this example in mind, let us now consider how this would work in spiritual matters.

The grantor of the trust is God, the trust document is Scripture, the beneficiary of God's provision is the steward, and the trustee is the pastor.

God has provided for us, the beneficiaries (the stewards), from His storehouse and has given us express instructions on how to use those provisions in His trust document (the Bible—over 2,350 verses). The trustee (the pastor) is charged with instructing us on how the trust God has set up for us is to be used so we will not violate God's trust document. He is to teach us the Word so that we will act in accordance with it and not violate it out of ignorance.

If we are in violation of God's will, the pastor is to point us to the trust document (Bible) and exhort us to comply with the directives as they are recorded in the document God has drafted. If we do not comply, it is not the pastor's responsibility to force us to do so, or to condemn us. The pastor's responsibility is to simply take us to the authority (God) and to leave us in His hands. God will administer the corrective action.

I knew of a pastor who asked to see the books of the flock he was shepherding. When he found someone who was not complying as he thought he or she should, he took corrective action. If the person did not respond, he encouraged the church to shun that individual in an effort to make him or her comply. (Yes, this is a true story in evangelical America!) He was in violation of God's trust agreement and overstepping his authority. He dealt with the situation instead of letting God do it, and ya know what happened? God dealt with Him! The fastest growing church in the city, the talk of the town closed its doors, and he is no longer a pastor. The beautiful building they renovated is now a lawyer's office. And God has appointed a new trustee for those stewards!

"Timothy, guard what has been entrusted to you!" This applies not only to finances but also to other areas. What kind of shepherd doesn't guard his flock and allows the financial wolves to get into the fold?

I implore you—do not turn your head and look the other way for any of the reasons given or for any other reason. The Church today has the educational resources available to it. Pastor/trustee, you must consider the state of your flock in the area of finances. Establish a financial ministry in your church and then watch the people and the ministry grow!

Let me caution the do-it-yourself, backyard-mechanic, Monday-morning-quarterback, "I am going to develop my own program" type of leader! Listen to me. Do you know what you are doing? You are starting out where the financial ministries were years ago, trying to find out what way works best to develop the financially faithful. So often a pastor will get someone in the church to put together a class, a seminar, a counseling program, and it is just not effective. I have been there and done that! That is why I am promoting programs that have years of experience, and have been proven effective because they have been fine-tuned because of that experience. I believe God has anointed them to bring about this change. It is best to deal with experts. Let them help you train your people so that you can become self-sufficient.

The Crown Financial Ministries small group study in tandem with the budget counselor program are the best way I have seen for a church to develop a financial help ministry. I do not get anything for promoting this program. I just know it is effective. I was developing my own small group study after a number of years of experience and conducting seminars and classes when I discovered these programs. At that time, God showed me that He had gone before me and prepared the way, and that I did not have to reinvent the wheel. When I combined the introduction of these programs with the Advancing the Kingdom Weekends I conduct, their effectiveness was incredible. The weekend messages provided the call to financial faithfulness to the stewards and the programs provided the method to implement that change.

So far in this book, we have seen how we can call a church or organization to financial faithfulness and how to equip them with what they need. Now let us take a look at a vision of the financially faithful Church.

CHAPTER 20

THE VISION OF THE FINANCIALLY FAITHFUL CHURCH

I magine the impact if the Church would get hold of the vision of the financially faithful Christian who is financially free to serve God, of people who not only retire from their career but retire early and then enter full-time Christian service, advancing the gospel of Jesus Christ. Now that is servanthood! That is effective ministry!

We as believers must not just *affect* society but *infect* the world for Christ. Proverbs 11:11 tells us that "by the blessing of the righteous, a city is exalted." Change always follows revival. The Renaissance followed the Reformation. The world will follow our example! But we cannot affect society if we are serving "mammon" or money. That is what the world serves. In doing so, we have become just like them. We cannot be a blessing unless we are blessed! We cannot be a leader unless we lead. We need to get our character, which should be a reflection of the Savior, into the world—not let the world's character get into us!

Would you dream with me in this chapter as we consider the possibilities that are before the Church today? The task before the local church is to discover how to handle money God's way so that the Christian individually and the Church corporately is financially free to serve the Lord.

The Church goes to great effort to teach the truths of the Scripture, so that Christians are equipped with the knowledge of the Word and its application to their life. In applying that Scripture to their life they become "salt and light" to the world. We send them out to "preach the gospel," but we forget that they are still tied to a financial ball and chain. They cannot focus; they become distracted, frustrated, and then ineffective in their ministry and in their walk.

Imagine what your church could do with people freed up to serve and with the revenues in the church treasury to supply the fuel for their expanded ministry.

In the light of the scriptural teaching found in this book, dream with me about the financially faithful Church and the faithful steward who is taught by the Word and not the world, and consider the following suppositions:

SUPPOSE...

Ten thousand of the Lord's money managers (that's you and 9,999 others) in your area reduce $10,000 of credit card debt which was held at 15-percent interest.

That's 10,000 X $10,000 which equals $100,000,000 in debt reduction!

The result...

There would be $15,000,000 per year of interest payments freed up to be given and used to advance the Master's Kingdom in your city or area alone!

Let's bring this example down to the level of your local church. Now I have indicated that the average Christian whom I have counseled is paying about $300 to $400 per month in credit or consumer credit interest. Let's assume that the average Christian in your church is not nearly that bad and only pays on the average $100-per-month interest. Let us also assume that your church has 200 adults in it and only 100 have credit cards. (Am I being conservative here or what?)

SUPPOSE...

One hundred people in your church eliminated $100-per-month interest payment on their credit cards and they gave that $100 to missions instead.

The result...

100 X $100 equals $10,000; that's $10,000 per month; $120,000-per-year increase in the missions' budget of the church.

(Do you remember I told you that the average Christian gives $20 per year to missions?)

Am I talking to anybody out there? Better yet, is the Master talking to anybody out there?

Let's talk some more! Better yet, let's let Him talk some more!

Consider the following fact as we look at another supposition:

In an average household, according to a government study, 35 percent of the household's income goes to meet interest payments, not including mortgage interest.

SUPPOSE...

Our average steward, who makes an annual income of $40,000, becomes obedient to biblical principles and becomes debt free.

The result...

Fourteen thousand dollars ($14,000) per year is freed up to meet the steward's full tithe ($4,000), to give over and above the tithe (offering—let's say giving $3,000) and still be able to save for the steward's future and the security of his family's finances. (Are you saving $7,000 per year and giving $7,000 per year?)

When you duplicate this steward's results over and over, with more stewards doing the same thing, the money the Master has put in the stewards' custody and care would have an incredibly great impact due to multiplication.

Consider the following, which is a realistic example.

SUPPOSE...

Ten thousand Christians in your city or area become debt free and give $10,000 per year to ministries.

The result...

10,000 X $10,000 equal $100,000,000!

That's a $100–million-a-year increase (I said increase) in gifts to ministries!

That's in *your* community!

Now here comes one that really blows my mind!

Do you remember how I told you that the financial planning industry estimates that 7 to 10 trillion dollars will change hands in the next 5 to 10 years as our senior generation passes down their wealth to the baby boomer generation? It has been estimated that 25 to 35 percent of that senior generation are Christians.

Very few of that generation has done adequate planning for the transfer of wealth, and unfortunately, much of it will go to pay taxes.

Suppose...

These Christians plan their estates considering the command by Christ to "be rich towards God" and gift 50 percent of their wealth to advance the Kingdom.

The result...

There would be an estimated $1.25 trillion (notice that this word has a "T" in it—you know, as in millions, billions, then trillions) that would pass into the hands of ministries within the next 5 to 10 years— now get this—*over and above current giving and tithing!*

Say, "Wow!" Now, say it backward! "Wow!"

Now just imagine what could be accomplished for the cause of Christ with that kind of money!

Now Suppose...

God's children begin to handle their money according to biblical principles, and the local church begins to run programs to teach biblical principles of finance to their members. They therefore begin to manage, save, and invest the money that the Lord has given them to take care of while He is away, and they do so with *moral, biblical* values. His stewards begin to use their Deuteronomy 8:18 power to accumulate wealth, and they invest and manage it in a way that allows them to be "salt and light" on the earth (see Matt. 5:13-14). They also combine their assets at a common financial institution, investing with biblical principles, and save and invest together for maximum Kingdom results.

The result…

The formation of the Kingdom Bank where Christians can become a formidable force, humanly speaking, infecting and affecting the world for Christ, funding the Great Commission, becoming the lender and not the borrower, advancing His Kingdom, and then ruling and reigning with Him as He sets up His Kingdom!

Politically speaking, the world is being set up for that final confrontation, and the Church must prepare financially to fund the end-time move of the Spirit.

You will be hearing more from me in the future on the Kingdom Bank. At the writing of this book, the vision of the Kingdom Bank is beginning to come together as Christian banking institutions, investment companies, financial planners, and financial training resources are being developed and come together to make Christ's glorious Church one of the most, if not the most, formidable financial forces in the world. (It's part of God's plan, as you will see in the last chapter.) We will become a formidable force as we begin to exercise our God-given authority, using our power of attorney to act in Jesus' name, and operate in God's financial principles recorded in that great Financial Manual, the Word of God. We will no longer conform to the world's financial systems, but with a renewed mind operate in the Word's financial systems (see Rom. 12:2).

Yes, all this is now within the grasp of the Church!

"Wow," you say, "where did this guy ever get a vision like this? Such a dreamer! Why is he spending his life in the effort to get this message to the Church?"

Now, let me assure you, I am no "holier than thou" person in this area. I said at the beginning of this book that I, of all people, feel I do not have the right to write such a book because I have made mistakes in all arenas of my life. Much of what I have learned, I have learned firsthand through life experiences, being in the battle trench myself, buried by debt. While I write this, my family continues to finally work our way out of the debt jungle, but praise God, we see freedom just ahead. If the Lord returned at this moment, I am sure I would still fall into the category of a "Brother Hanky" for sure. So you see, this is also for me! I also want to become a "president" in Christ's Kingdom!

Hey, the Lord has put me in reform school, and I am recruiting other students to go with me. Will you come?

Ernest Hemmingway once said, "Now is not the time to think of what you do not have; think of what you can do with what there is." We cannot focus on the past and what we have done wrong or what we do not have. We must take a look at where we are and what we must do to change that, and then move to action! Remember faith becomes a verb when we come to Christ and we must take action! We cannot wait until things are right in order to serve the Lord. And they never seem to get right while we wait anyway. Remember the cause of paralysis in Chapter 4 and the way out? Review those steps again:

Faith—action with conviction!

Effort—discipline and obedience.

Education—can't do it if we don't know how

and

Accountability—the Master is coming back!

How has His Kingdom fared with those things He has given to you to take care of while He was away?

Let me share an event with you from my life and perhaps you will understand why I have such a vision.

I identify with the Apostle Paul in Second Corinthians 12 where he says in verse 2, "Whether it was in the body or out of the body, I do not know—God knows."

I too was caught up into paradise, where I heard inexpressible things that I am unable to tell. However, there are some things that I believe I am commanded to tell.

It was during emergency surgery in 1995, that I felt myself in the presence of Christ Himself. The surgery was one in which I almost did not make it through, and when I did, my wife was told there were no promises that I would continue to make it through the coming night.

In this "near-death experience," as the world calls it (I prefer to call it a life experience, I was never more alive!), the Lord talked with me about this very issue—the need for the Church to become financially faithful, and He charged me to take this message to the Church.

During the subsequent months of recovery as well as a second extensive surgery, I began, in more depth, to study His Word on the subject and lay the groundwork for the ministry and what eventually became this book. I did not realize at the time what I was doing, but as I look back, I now see that path clearly. During that period, I wrestled with the validity and truth of the experience, tried to pass it off as imagination, and even blamed the morphine I had been given for pain, but it didn't work. I even went through a period of rebellion against it, as I saw some of the things I knew in the Spirit (but could not tell others) begin to unfold in the reality of life.

Some things were insignificant to anyone but me. Other things had wider significance, like the merger of Crown Ministries and Christian Financial Concepts into Crown Financial Ministries. Christ has consolidated His forces in this area as He said He would. One year before Larry Burkett ever approached Howard Dayton about merging the ministries, I in response to the Body's perceived competition of these two ministries, heard myself respond to my wife something I could only know in the Spirit. I said, "Well, it is only a matter of time before those two become one." The merger was further evidence that the rest of the experience was real and that God is preparing to move in a big way in the area of the finances of the Church. *Yes, God does not need our money (it's already His!), but He needs our obedience, our focus, and our time to carry out His plan. Our use of money is the evidence of our obedience and faith.* He has always used Israel or the Church and the systems, governmental and monetary, to carry out His plans. That is what He is doing here, and He wants you to be an active part of His plan.

Let me share with you something that the Lord said to me while in the midst of this experience, of which I have received many confirmations. I will preface this by telling you that in the context of what occurred, I believe that the word "fuel" refers to money or finances.

The Lord said to me: *"If My people will be about My business and begin to gather together the fuel to fund the end-time move of My Spirit…"*

The Lord said…

"I'll light the match!"

Stewards!

I believe…

these words…

are red!

CHAPTER *21*

HOLE-Y PURSES!

I want us to look at another passage in our Financial Manuals—in the Book of Haggai. You remember this Book, don't you? It is that obscure book at the end of the Old Testament, the one that you always got confused with Habbakuk when you were learning to recite the books of the Bible in Sunday school. Unfortunately, for most of us, that is all we know about the second shortest book in the Old Testament.

I was first introduced to Haggai in my "Post-Exilic Prophets" class in my final year as a ministerial student at Houghton College. I learned that Haggai was a prophet, who along with his friend and contemporary, Zechariah the prophet, encouraged the returned exiles to rebuild the temple under Zerubbabel's leadership.

I encourage you to read this book. Haggai's teaching shows the consequences of disobedience and obedience, and he specifically addresses finances.

Now, I especially don't like to talk about that obedience stuff. It is against my nature! While I was growing up, my parents used a yardstick for spankings when I was disobedient. (I look at that stick today and wonder why I was so terrified.) And...well...let me put it this way—my backside racked up more yardage than Walter Payton, Emmett Smith, or any other NFL running back has ever gained in their career! They eat my dust!

However, there are rewards in obedience, and Haggai clearly teaches that if we are obedient to God's principles, blessings will result. Remember that I said for the believer, *obedience* and *prosperity* mean the same thing. It is from Haggai's message that I have developed what I call the five "P's" of financial planning. Consider Haggai 1:4-6,9:

"Is it a time for you yourselves to be living in your paneled houses, while this house remains a ruin?" Now this is what the Lord Almighty says: "Give careful thought to your ways. You have planted much, but have harvested little. You eat, but never have enough. You drink, but never have your fill. You put on clothes, but are not warm. You earn wages, only to put them in a purse with holes in it.... You expected much, but see, it turned out to be little. What you brought home, I blew away! Why?" declares the Lord Almighty. "Because of My house, which remains a ruin, while each of you is busy with his own house" (emphasis added).

Sound familiar? Some things don't change, whether it is the 21st century or 520 B.C.

Let us back up for a minute and consider what was happening.

Zerubbabel had led a group of exiled Jews back to Jerusalem to rebuild the temple. They arrived and were busily going about getting their finances, living arrangements, businesses, and family life in order. And they were waiting for the right time to start to build the house of the Lord.

Then God spoke to Haggai the prophet and told him to go to the leadership and to the people and tell them that they had been so busy with their own affairs that they neglected the work that God had called them to do. He also told them that it was for this reason they were not being blessed and the labor of their hands was not bearing fruit.

This passage reminds me of Philippians 2:21 where Paul tells the Philippians that "everyone looks out for their own interests, not those of Jesus Christ."

The Church today could be incredibly powerful if God's people would become financially faithful and be about God's business to advance the Kingdom, to build His house. If we would faithfully invest in the Kingdom, *the devil would tremble in fear every time the offering plate was passed!*

I say, let's scare the tar out of old slew foot!

Pass the plate and deal him his fate!

How does satan react when the plate reaches you?

Are you intimidated by the plate, or do you intimidate through the plate?

I like to say, *the offering basket is the devil's casket!*

How about your church? Are you just meeting the bills, or are you affecting your community for Christ?

Unfortunately, right now, for the most part, *we are earning wages only to put them in a purse with holes in it.* The money falls out and is picked up by credit card companies, consumer loan companies, and other creditors. When we look in the purse, we wonder where the money went, and we worry. We lose our focus and then begin to serve money rather than God.

This passage goes on to say that when the Jews heard the message, they obeyed. In verse 14 we read that the "Lord stirred up the spirit" of Zerubbabel and of Joshua the high priest. These guys were the leaders, and for change to occur in any church or organization, the leadership must get stirred up first. "So the Lord stirred up the spirit of Zerubbabel...and the spirit of Joshua...and the spirit of the whole remnant of the people. They came and began to work on the house of the Lord Almighty, their God" (Hag.1:14).

The leaders must be stirred up to do something about the finances of the church, both individually and corporately. Once the leaders get stirred up, then the church can be stirred up. Then hang on and watch God work! Watch Him work in individual lives and families and in their personal ministries, and watch Him work in the overall ministry of the Church.

How about it, pastor, church leader, steward? Have you been apathetic to developing a financial ministry in your church?

You don't want Haggai knocking on your door with a message from God, do you?

Well, I must tell you, however, if you have just read this, God just sent a message! No, He didn't send Haggai, but He did send Buck.

Am I talking to anyone out there?

So, what about the five "P's" I mentioned I would share with you?

Haggai told God's people that because they were so busy with their own affairs, they were neglecting the work that God had called them to do. Consequently, they were not being blessed. So Haggai chose to #1: *Prod* them to do something, to take corrective action about their situation, to identify the problem. Once they have been prodded into corrective action, Haggai then moved them to #2: *Prioritize* what they were doing and be about God's business first. In this instance, God's business was to rebuild the temple and they were to #3: *Plan* their course of action to rectify the problem. They then began to #4: *Prepare* by gathering together the materials and the manpower to rebuild the temple and by obeying the command of God. God then promised them that if they were focusing on His business instead of on their own, He would #5: *Prosper* them.

How do the five "P's" work for us today?

1. *Prod*: We should prod ourselves into taking corrective action. We must identify our financial problem and decide to do something about it. Maybe our only problem is that we don't recognize that "our" money is God's, and that we are not "being rich towards Him" with it. Our circumstances, an experience of a friend, a speaker, or even this book might cause you to be prodded or poked by the Holy Spirit to take action.

2. *Prioritize*: Set your priorities. What is important for you to see happen in your life and in your finances in the coming year? Do you need to establish a budget, a debt reduction program, or do some retirement or estate planning? Perhaps you should evaluate your life insurance program or fine-tune your budget. Maybe you should develop a money management program or make an appointment for professional assistance in your financial plan. Maybe you should enroll in a stewardship training program. Write your priorities down. Remember Haggai's message and ask yourself: Am I so concerned about my own affairs of home and finances that I am neglecting the work of the Master's Kingdom?

3. *Plan*: Have you developed a financial plan? Do you know what your goals are? Where is your focus? Financially speaking, where do you want to be a year from now, five years from now, or at retirement age? How exactly are you going to get out of debt? Your financial plan must

be written to be effective so it can be reviewed and changed as circumstances change.

4. *Prepare*: Do you have a budget? Are you tithing? What is your attitude toward money? Are you saving or hoarding? How are you investing in the Kingdom? Are you investing like the world dictates or as the Word commands? Are you unknowingly supporting things with your investments that are contrary to Scripture? Now go and find the necessary information and help that you need to implement your plan. Make that telephone call! Pray and seek the Holy Spirit's guidance as you implement your plan and take your God-given authority over your finances.

5. *Prosper*: This is the fun part—the rewards of obedience! God promises to bless us when we turn from disobedience to obedience to God's principles. "From this day on I will bless you" (Hag. 2:19). We need to be obedient to God's will in all things in order to be in God's blessing cycle.

Perhaps Haggai's message is best summed up in the words of the Master Himself (Jesus) in Matthew 6:33 (red words again folks!): "Seek ye first the Kingdom of God, and His righteousness, and all these things will be added unto you" (KJV).

Don't be like the unnamed believers in Philippians 2:21 of which Paul said, "For everyone looks out for his own interests, not those of Jesus Christ." Start out with a new day regardless of your past or how hopeless the future appears; be exhorted to become a financially faithful servant and a financially faithful Church. Let us get on with the Kingdom's business!

What are we waiting for? There is a great move of the Spirit in the area of finances in the Church today. The revolution has begun! Is your church missing it? More importantly, are you missing it?

Listen!

We can keep running through that sticker bush I talked about in the first chapter—thinking that if we go faster and faster, things might change. We can keep letting the thorns or the cares of life tear at us and at our ministries, or we can stop and be obedient to the One who has already taken those thorns for us as a crown and turned it into a crown of life—abundant life!

Job 36:11 says, "If they obey and serve Him, they will spend the rest of their days in prosperity and their years in contentment."

Think about it! Not too long though.

The Master is waiting for your answer!

There is work to be done! We've got to start building the house of the Lord! Join the revolution now!

The Master expects it!

He's coming back!

Excited?

Well, it all can be summed up in two verses of the Bible. Please read on and learn about them in the next final chapter. Then sign on to join the financial revolution in the Church. Literally sign the last page of the next chapter and mail it to us, stating that you are standing with us in this end-time mighty work of the Spirit.

CHAPTER 22

TWO VERSES

When God called me to start a financial revolution in the Church of Christ in order to fund the Great Commission given by Jesus, I knew that there was an issue that He had to settle with me first so that I could adequately operate in the anointing to which He had called me during a "near-death experience." I knew a difficult and long road lay ahead in changing the way I had conducted things in the past, and I struggled with two verses in the Bible that I wished were not there. Just like Jacob who wrestled with the angel of the Lord and said, "I will not let go until you bless me," I said, "I will not let go until you answer me!"

Proverbs 15:6 says, "In the house of the righteous there is much treasure" (NKJV); and Proverbs 13:22b says, "The wealth of the sinner is stored up for the righteous" (NKJV).

Now understand, I liked the sound of those verses for I, because of Jesus, counted myself among the righteous, but frankly, they did not reflect what I saw happening in the Body of Christ. I saw a lot of blood-bought, redeemed-by-the-Lamb children of God who didn't have much treasure in their house and were struggling to make ends meet. I saw ministry leaders pleading for assistance but still being a dollar short and a day late in accomplishing what God had called them to do. *Debt had taken the place of treasure!* And while the righteous lacked, I saw the wicked prospering. I wondered why Solomon, who was supposed to have possessed God-given wisdom, would say something so dumb!

Jesus told me, "I will answer your question, and you will answer these and many other questions of the Church in regard to finances." He then proceeded with an explanation; one verse was simply a statement of fact, and the other...prophetic!

Jesus went on to point out that when Solomon declared that "in the house of the righteous, there is much treasure"…it was true! It has been estimated that during the reign of King Solomon, 85 to 90 percent of the world's wealth was in the hands of God's people, the nation of Israel. God had covenanted with their father, Abraham, that He would bless them. Many years later, Jesus said that although they possessed all this wealth, because of and through their disobedience, Israel gave it back to the world! He then said to me, "My treasure is now mostly in alien hands."

He went on to explain that because of the promise of the Father and because of Jesus' sacrifice on Calvary, that same covenant God made with Abraham now extends to His Church, the "joint heirs" in the inheritance of all that the Father has to give. The other verse, Proverbs 13:22 is the prophetic one. He said, "The wealth of the sinner [or as some versions call it, the wealth of the world] is stored up for [or is coming into the hands of) the righteous." Jesus said to me that it was *His* intention to bring *His* wealth back into the hands of *His* people to fund the end-time move of *His* Spirit and bring about *His* Kingdom. He said that ministry leaders will be able to focus on ministry issues and not funding issues. The money will begin to flow as *His* Church begins to walk in financial faithfulness; they then will accumulate and invest *His* wealth in *His* Kingdom.

Read that last paragraph again!

We are told in various places throughout the Scripture that God intends to bring the wealth of the world back into the hands of His people. Remember, because of Christ, God's promises to Abraham and the nation of Israel now extend to the Church. Consider, with this fact in mind, the following passages:

For this is what the Lord Almighty says: In just a little while I will again shake the heavens and the earth. I will shake the oceans and the dry land, too. I will shake all the nations, and the treasures of all the nations will come to this Temple. I will fill this place with glory, says the Lord Almighty. The silver is mine, and the gold is mine, says the Lord Almighty. The future glory of this Temple will be greater than its past glory, says the Lord Almighty. And in this place I will bring peace. I, the Lord Almighty, have spoken! (Haggai 2:6-9 NLT)

Powerful kings and mighty nations will bring the best of their goods to satisfy your every need. You will know at last that I, the Lord, am your Savior and Redeemer, the Mighty One of Israel. I will exchange your bronze for gold, your iron for silver, your wood for bronze, and your stones for iron. Peace and righteousness will be your leaders! Violence will disappear from your land; the desolation and destruction of war will end. Salvation will surround you like city walls, and praise will be on the lips of all who enter there (Isaiah 60:16-18 NLT).

It still gives me chills every time I remember these words He spoke to me…

"Just as My people Israel, through *disobedience* to My commands, gave My wealth to the world, the Church now through *obedience* to the Word will get it back!" He then said, "If My people will be about My business, and gather together the fuel to fund the end-time move of My Spirit…I'll light the match!"

The problem is that the Church has been taught by the world and not the Word. They have conformed to the world's systems and methods, and not God's. They know little about the second-most talked about subject in the Bible…money and possessions. They need to learn biblical principles for handling the 90 percent, not just the 10 percent, enabling them to tap into their Deuteronomy 8:18 promise: "power to gain wealth." Presently they plant seeds and God multiplies it back, but because they lack *knowledge*, they eat their new seed. I have always said that Christians are too much like birds…they eat seeds!

Consider this: The more the Church walks in obedience, the more wealth it will accumulate to accomplish Christ's purpose; God will need to "cash in" more of the world's wealth so He can be faithful to fulfill His promise. As we become financially free to serve Him, the Lord will command the world to give up the wealth (as in the exodus from Egypt) and command us to use it to take us to the Promised Land…this time, His Kingdom!

He told me that ministry leaders need "to plant seeds of financial faithfulness" in their congregations, donors, and partners in order to reap a greater harvest as the King's treasury begins to fill up. They are to do this by providing ways for them to learn His principles regarding money and possessions as taught in the Scriptures. They need to not only know how to plant seeds, but also cultivate new seeds and then maintain and harvest the crop. Educating the steward needs to be a primary focus of ministries as we expect the soon arrival of Christ's coming Kingdom. We need to learn not only how to get the wealth of the world back into the Master's hands for *His* purposes, but also how to keep it!

My People are gone into captivity, because they have no knowledge (Isaiah 5:13a KJV).

Carefully follow the terms of the covenant, so that you may prosper in everything you do (Deuteronomy 29:9 NIV).

God bless you all...Shalom! Nothing missing, nothing broken.

APPENDIX

INDUCTION PAPERS

Please complete this page and mail to the address below. In turn, we will send resources to help you start a revolution not only in your own life but at your local church level or in your community.

Buck,

Please sign me on as one who will join forces with other fellow believers in the financial revolution of God's people. Please keep me informed of ways that I can become financially faithful and handle the money entrusted to me by Christ in an eternally significant way. I pledge to support the revolution by learning and practicing biblical principles and to actively recruit other believers to do the same.

Signed: _____

Name _____

Address: _____

_____

Email Address _____

Phone: _____

Are you a financial advisor? _____
Registered with whom? _____

While reading this book, I made a decision to be part of God's family. Please send me information on how I can know Him better. _____(please check)

Send to: Buck Stephens
              Advancing the Kingdom Ministries
              PO Box 274
              Syracuse, New York 13214

Don't Stop Reading Yet!

Author's Note: Andrea and I both were deeply affected by the following teaching written by one of the great teachers of our time. As I look back over the years, I recognize that reading this book was what started my thinking as a young husband, father, and financial advisor to desire a more excellent way when it comes to financial matters. That more excellent way, as you have read in my book, is based upon the Scriptures. Reading *The Miracle of Seed Faith*, by Oral Roberts, may have been the first step that led me to write this book and to this point in my life and ministry. Since that time, I have encountered many other lives that have also been touched by the teaching of *The Miracle of Seed Faith*.

I encourage you to read this shortened version of Oral Roberts' book, reprinted on the following pages, and I strongly encourage you to obtain a copy of the entire book. I want to thank Richard Roberts and Oral Roberts for allowing us to include a portion of this book that has affected the lives of so many over the years. I believe it to be a valuable asset for the coming revolution.

To obtain a copy of this book, send $7.00 along with your name and address to:

Oral Roberts Evangelistic Association

7777 S. Lewis Avenue

Tulsa, Oklahoma 74171-10000

You may also order online from the Abundant Life Bookstore at
www.orm.cc

THE MIRACLE OF SEED FAITH

There are times in our lives when nothing less than a miracle will do. We all face mountains of needs—physical problems, financial problems, spiritual problems, fear of what's going to happen to us and our loved ones, fear of whether we're going to make it or not. We all need a miracle.

A miracle doesn't happen by chance. You help to generate a miracle by doing what God says—by planting your faith like a seed so you can reap miracles, by opening your mind to God, and by learning to use your faith in a definite scriptural way.

When you put your faith in God's hands like a seed you plant, you are giving God something to work with, and He will send the miracle.

People often ask me how we have accomplished the things that we have in this ministry. Usually I answer, "By faith." When they say, "Be more specific," I say, "By living and practicing the three miracle keys of Seed-Faith."

Those miracle keys are:

1. God is your Source (Philippians 4:19).

2. Give that it may be given unto you (Luke 6:38).

3. Expect a miracle (Mark 11:24).

These miracle keys of Seed-Faith have become so real and personal that they are a way of life for me. I've tested them against every type of need and problem, both spiritual and material, and they work. They've never failed me.

When I've had no earthly source or person to turn to, when I've been alone with nothing but big problems and challenges facing me, these principles have shown me that God is my Source. They show me how to use my giving as a seed I plant, and to expect God to multiply it even if it takes a miracle.

How I Discovered the Miracle of Seed-Faith

One day in 1954 I was driving along in the northwestern part of the United States and thinking about all my problems and needs. I glanced over as I drove and saw the great harvest fields and the big trucks hauling the grain and fruit to market.

It suddenly occurred to me that somebody had planted a seed, somebody had reaped a harvest, and somebody had gathered the harvest and was taking it to town to sell. They were receiving their money and they were buying the things to meet their needs and they were coming back home to plant another crop. As I saw all of this happening, I began to understand what I'd been reading in the Bible.

I became conscious for the first time that in everything I do, I am planting a seed—not of grain, but a seed of faith. I'd planted seeds of faith before, but hadn't realized it.

Oral Roberts University is the result of some of that seed planting— some of my harvest. So is the CityPlex Towers Complex. Every building on the ORU campus is the result of thousands of my partners who learned to plant their seeds and to receive their harvest not only here but also in their own lives. Many of my partners have children who are going to ORU, or who have graduated from here, or who plan to come here. There are parents all over this country who have received miracles through this ministry. But every one of them can point back to where they started planting seeds of faith and expecting miracles.

Everything Starts with a Seed

Everything starts with a seed. In Genesis 8:22 God says:

"While the earth remaineth, seed-time and harvest...shall not cease."

I like to call this SEEDTIME and HARVESTTIME, which means GIVING and RECEIVING. God says this eternal law will not change as long as the earth remains!

St. Paul referred to this eternal law of sowing and reaping in Galatians 6:

"Whatsoever a man soweth, that shall he also reap. And let us not be weary in well doing: for in due season we shall reap, if we faint not" (Galatians 6:7, 9).

Jesus constantly likened faith to a seed being planted to get a result. He said:

"If ye have faith as a grain of mustard seed, ye shall say unto this mountain, Remove hence to yonder place; and it shall remove" (Matthew 17:20).

If you have faith as a seed, or if your believing becomes SEED-FAITH, no matter how small it seems to be, it will meet needs and problems that appear as impossible to move as mountains before you. This is because each act of faith is a seed planted and will be multiplied many times.

THE FIRST MIRACLE KEY OF SEED-FAITH IS:
GOD IS YOUR SOURCE

"My God shall supply all your need according to his riches in glory by Christ Jesus" (Philippians 4:19).

Many times when people face a problem, they go to pieces because they don't know who their Source is. Philippians 4:19 gives us the answer: "*GOD* shall supply all your need." God is concerned about your life, and He wants you to RECEIVE from His hand. But He wants you to recognize Him as your SOURCE OF RECEIVING.

Now what does this really mean? It simply means that GOD IS YOUR SOURCE OF TOTAL SUPPLY.

GOD will supply ALL your needs. And He will supply them not depending on the economy being good, or depending on your business or your job. Your supply comes from God your source according to His riches, His love for you, His power to help you, His wisdom to guide you.

God is bigger than any or all your needs put together...and He cannot fail. He may use many different instruments—a job, gifts, doctors, friends—to meet your need. But HE alone is the SOURCE...and He alone cannot fail.

You may lose your job. But you can get another job. You can become disenchanted with your church or lose confidence in your friends. But if your life is grounded in your Source—God—you will heal and mend, and you will live and continue to multiply and be a fruitful individual.

Friend, it makes all the difference in the world who your Source is. Your Source is not a what, it's a WHO. My Source is not a what, it's a WHO. God in me is my Source. Your Source. Our Source.

My Uncle's Orchard

While I was growing up we lived close to an uncle who made his living from his big orchard. He was the one who first helped me see the difference between source and instrument. He raised all kinds of fruit, but his pride and joy was the big luscious Elberta peach. People came from miles to buy his peaches.

I moved away, and it was several years before I visited my uncle again. I was shocked when I saw his orchard...or what remained of it. Only a few of the prized peach trees remained; they were scrubby and produced only a few small peaches.

"What happened?" I asked my uncle. "Did you have a storm? Or was it insects?"

Sadly he replied, "Oral, I simply did not pay attention to the trees. The fruit fed my family. I depended upon the fruit as the source of my supply.

"Then one year the crop was not so good; the next year it was less. I woke up and realized that the source of my supply was the tree...not the fruit! I saw that if I took care of the tree, the fruit would grow." Then his eyes lighted up. "I'm putting in a new orchard. This time I'll take care of my source."

God is your Source of total supply just as the tree is the source of the fruit. If you cultivate your relationship with God—look to Him and trust Him—the supply of your needs and the answer to your prayer will come because God as Source controls the harvest.

THE SECOND MIRACLE KEY OF SEED-FAITH IS: GIVE THAT IT MAY BE GIVEN UNTO YOU

"Give [first], and it shall be given unto you" (Luke 6:38).

The second step of Seed-Faith—planting a seed so God can multiply it back to meet your need—is the one that more people stumble over than any other. All our lives we've been taught to give...and to give freely...but NOT to expect to receive anything in return. In fact, we've been taught that it's a sin to expect to receive something back when we give. But Jesus himself clearly said:

"Give [first], and it SHALL be given unto you; good measure, pressed down, and shaken together, and running over, shall men give into your bosom. For with the same measure that ye mete withal it shall be measured to you again" (Luke 6:38).

You see, there is no way you can give to God without *receiving something back*...MULTIPLIED! God can't do otherwise or He would be going against His own eternal law of sowing and reaping.

What you give is a seed of faith you plant, and the seed you put in God multiplies back...to help others and also to meet your own needs (2 Corinthians 9:10).

It's a whole new way of life. It is giving God something to work with. You sow it and God will grow it.

Jesus said, "It is more blessed [more productive] to give than to receive" (Acts 20:35). Why? Because God has put receiving into giving. It is like the yeast in bread. The dough is not multiplied until the yeast in it becomes the multiplying agent of that which you give. Your giving ties you to God. It links you to His inexhaustible resources.

Give God something to work with. No matter how little you think you have, sow it first...in joy and faith, knowing in your heart that you are seeding so you may reap miracles. Then start expecting all kinds of miracles.

The idea of seeding for your miracle is based on God's eternal law of seedtime and harvest (Genesis 8:22). It is giving and receiving. Seeding for your miracle is giving first...or thanking God in advance. It is like the grace you say before meals. You are giving thanks before the object of your thanks has been received into your mouth—as if it already had been received. It is an act of seed-planting, an act of faith, of giving and expecting a return just as the farmer does at harvest time.

HE WANTS YOU, NOT JUST YOUR MONEY

When we use the word *give*, most people just think of dollars and cents. But God doesn't want *just* your money. He wants YOU! (1 Corinthians 6:19, 20).

Seed-giving takes many forms and represents your TOTAL SELF. Jesus is talking in Luke 6:38 about giving in the deepest sense of the word...*the giving of yourself.* It includes your earnings but it is not limited to that. Jesus also included other important forms of giving which involve one's spirit or one's self: the giving of seed-love, seed-time, seed-patience, seed-forgiveness, a seed-smile. Give as a seed what you need to receive.

If you need love, give love.

If you are out of time, give some time.

If you want friendship desperately, that's what you give.

If you need money to pay your bills, take some of what you have and give it to our Lord and His work.

A smile can be a seed of faith. So can a kind word, or just a touch.

Recently a man walked up to me and put his hand on my shoulder and gave me a gentle pat. "Oral," he said, "you're doing a great work for God."

He didn't know it, but that day I was so low that if I had died they would have had to jack me up to bury me. That little touch on my shoulder and his encouraging words lifted me up.

You never know what happens to your gifts...how much God uses them. Though my friend was probably unaware of it, he was able to give me that day the very thing I needed most—encouragement. I know God met his need in return.

PLANT YOUR BEST SEED

The real heart of Seed-Faith is found in John 3:16:

"For God so loved the world, that he gave his only begotten Son, that whosoever believeth in him should not perish, but have everlasting life."

God so loved us that He gave...unconditionally. He made His love an act of giving. He planted a seed. Jesus Christ is said to be the seed of David (Matthew 1:1). God describes Christ as a seed (Genesis 3:15) and God planted that seed. God gave His best for us, as unworthy as we are, as unlovely as we are. He gave His only begotten Son. *He planted His best Seed.*

My daddy taught me to always plant the best seed. He was a preacher, but he was also a farmer until I was about 14 years old when he entered full-time ministry. And my brother Vaden and I always helped Papa with the crops.

One day we were gathering corn, pulling the corn off the stalk and throwing it into the wagon. We'd drive to the barn and we'd take shovels to pitch the ears of corn up into the barn as fast as we could because we hated farm work.

But one day Papa stopped us and said, "Wait a minute, Oral, Vaden, you're doing it wrong. Separate the corn. Look for the big ears, and put them over here in a pile on the ground and put the others in the barn.

Vaden and I didn't know any better. We said, "Papa, why?"

He said, "We never eat our seed corn. We save the best and plant that next year. We plant our best corn and we eat the other corn." I did not know the value of his advice until years later.

Don't ever eat your seed corn. *Give God your seed corn—your best seed—because that's what God multiplies.*

Do you realize that what you give to God is always multiplied, whether it's good or bad? If you give Him a bad seed, that's what He's got to multiply. If you give Him a good seed, that's what He's got to multiply.

GIVE FOR A DESIRED RESULT

God not only gave His best, He gave for a purpose—

"...that whosoever believeth in him should not perish, but have everlasting life."

God focused His giving. He initiated an action that would cause a desired result. And the desired result was that people who were lost would be saved...people who were in need would get their needs met.

God himself set the pattern for our giving. He showed us when we give, we can give as a seed we plant and we can direct our giving. We can focus it toward an object...or a particular return. We can say, "God, I have this need, and I am giving this seed-gift...I am directing it...toward the meeting of this need." And we can expect God to do it.

GIVE OUT OF YOUR NEED

God gave out of His need. The first time I realized this as I studied the Scripture, I thought, God doesn't have any needs. He's God. And then it came to me that God created man, and the devil stole man away. And God could never be satisfied and fulfilled until man is restored to Him. Until you and I are saved, God is not fulfilled.

God had a need and God gave out of His need. So did the poor widow in Mark 12:41-44:

"And Jesus sat over against the treasury, and beheld how the people cast money into the treasury: and many that were rich cast in much. And there came a certain poor widow, and she threw in two mites, which make a farthing [a couple of pennies]. And he called unto him his disciples, and saith unto them, Verily I say unto you, That this poor widow hath cast more in, than all they which have cast into the treasury [which was impossible]."

Many who were there that day gave a lot of money. They were rich and she was poor, so she gave only a little bit. They gave out of their abundance but she gave of her need, of her want. She gave of her living. She gave out of her need.

Now that's different from the way you and I have been taught. We've been taught to give the tithe, the tenth. We've been taught that when we earn ten dollars we should give the tenth dollar. This is Old Testament living. We've never been taught to give the first dollar for God to multiply.

GIVE NOT AS A DEBT YOU OWE BUT AS A SEED YOU SOW

In the Old Testament you received first, *then* you gave. To teach His ownership, God did things for people and after they received they were to give back to Him. It was a debt...they *owed* it to God. They owed God their time—the Sabbath. They owed Him money—the tithe. Everything was something they *owed* to God.

But the debt was insurmountable; man could not pay it, so God sent His Son Jesus to pay the debt. Jesus went to the cross and paid our debt by giving himself.

It is a completed work. You can't add to it. Therefore you can't do something and say, "I'm paying God." Jesus paid the price—He paid it *all.*

So now you give as a seed you sow. It is giving to receive. This is a whole new dimension of love and giving...a new framework of living! You can no longer give to God to pay a debt because Christ has already paid it. You come out of the Old Testament with its heavy requirements into the joy of New Testament living.

THE THIRD MIRACLE KEY OF SEED-FAITH IS: EXPECT A MIRACLE

"Therefore I say unto you, What things soever ye desire, when ye pray, believe that ye receive them, and ye shall have them" (Mark 11:24).

Just as you look TO God for your total supply and give TO God as a seed you sow, you also expect a miracle FROM God. This is the key on which many people fail in their Seed-Faith giving. They say, "Brother Roberts, I thought when you give to God it would be presumptuous to expect anything back."

Let me ask you—would a farmer sow seed if he didn't expect the miracle of a harvest? Every farmer I know goes to the field regularly to see how much the seed has grown. If he didn't expect a return, he wouldn't check his fields. And if he didn't check the fields, the harvest would come and he wouldn't know it. Thus it would be wasted.

The Scripture says:

"For God, who gives seed to the farmer to plant, and later on, good crops to harvest and eat, will give you more and more seed to plant and will make it grow so that you can give away more and more fruit from you harvest" (2 Corinthians 9:10, TLB).

FAITH HOLDS OUT A HAND

A friend said to me, "Oral, sometimes I think people believe in coke machines more than they believe in God."

"What do you mean?" I asked.

"Well, we put our coins into the coke machine and reach for a coke," he said. "But we ask God for something and just go about our business and don't act like we're expecting. We don't put out our hand to receive anything."

You know, he has a point there. I believe we should be so eager and ready to accept what God has for us that the moment we ask for something we would reach out our hand to accept it.

My wife, Evelyn, does this. After she has planted a seed of faith and has asked God to meet a need, every time the phone rings or the postman comes, she says to herself, "Is this my miracle?" Every time she meets someone, she asks, "Lord, are You using this person to bring my miracle?"

The moment you ask God for something, believe that it's coming and look for it. Dare to reach out your hand of faith to take what God has promised.

When you do your part and release your faith, God will send the miracle you need. This is your harvest. It is important to expect it so you will recognize your miracle when God sends it and reach forth and receive it from His hand.

You have a miracle coming toward you every day, or it is passing by you every day. Therefore, you must expect. Expect a miracle. Look for your miracle. Look for it to happen.

THE MIRACLE OF THE DUE SEASON

For some, this third step—learning to expect your miracle from God—is the most difficult part of Seed-Faith to practice. Because when you've done something good, you want something good to happen to you right away. And if it doesn't, it's hard to keep expecting your miracle from God.

If you're like me, you'll try to tell God HOW to give to you, WHEN to give to you, WHERE to give to you, and WHAT to give to you. But you don't control the "due season." God does. He alone holds your Seed-Faith in His hands. When you plant a seed, trust God for the harvest. No matter how long it takes, keep trusting God.

When Seed-Faith does not seem to be working for me, I find that it helps to check myself against the three principles of Seed-Faith:

First, am I looking to God as my Source of help? Or am I looking to man? (Philippians 4:19).

Second, is God really first in my life and my giving? Am I giving as an act of faith? (Luke 6:38).

Third, am I releasing my faith and living in expectancy? (Mark 11:24).

My giving doesn't bring the miracle. Giving is my point of contact to release my faith for the miracle to start.

Galatians 6:9 tells us that we should not be weary in well doing, "for in due season we shall reap, if we faint not." Your due season may come today or a year from now. It may come in the form of money or in the form of something money can't buy—a healing, a restored relationship, a spiritual blessing. You don't know just how or when it will come. But remember, God always sends the harvest at the RIGHT TIME, in the RIGHT WAY. His due season is always exactly right for your life.

SEED-FAITH IS A WAY OF LIFE

Seed-Faith cannot be a onetime thing...a gift that you give to suddenly make everything all right. No, Seed-Faith is a way of life. It is giving until giving becomes your life-style...until you become a disciple, a learner, a follower of Christ. You love and give...love and give...love and give.

You think it...

feel it...

experience it...

talk it...

do it.

True Seed-Faith begins with the need you have! It brings you into an involvement with Jesus Christ until you truly follow Him and become His disciple.

Become a giver in every area of your life. Get into Seed-Faithing—loving and giving—and you'll reap MIRACLE after MIRACLE after MIRACLE for the rest of your life.

A SEED-FAITH PRAYER FOR YOUR MIRACLE

Now I want to pray with you to expect a miracle and to see God change things in your existence. As I pray for you, I want you to pray for somebody else. One of the best ways to release your faith—to plant it as a seed —is to pray for someone else (James 5:16).

Father, in the name of Your Son Jesus, in the name of Jesus who rose from the dead, I ask for many miracles today...for miracles of life and deliverance.

And now, dear friend, I pray that Jesus Christ, the Son of God, will change your life, that you will experience a miracle of life itself.

I pray that Jesus Christ will take that pain you have and move it out, that He will take that problem you have and solve it...that Jesus Christ will take that need you have and meet it, that He will forgive your sins and wash them away by His shed blood and make you a new creature...that Jesus Christ will set you free from every bondage and make you a whole person from your head to your feet.

Through Christ I pray, I believe, and I expect a harvest of many miracles in your life. Amen and amen.

The End

No, it's not!

It's only the beginning of what God is going to do with your life!

For booking and information:

Contact

Buck Stephens

Advancing the Kingdom Ministries

PO Box 274

Syracuse, New York 13214

315-424-6180

or

Email: atkm@atkministries.org

www.atkministries.org

Schedule an Advancing the Kingdom Weekend
at your church or organization
with
Buck Stephens

DEVELOPING THE FINANCIALLY FAITHFUL CHURCH

The Crown Financial Ministries Small Group study has proven to be an effective tool in teaching biblical principles of finance to God's people, and the Advancing the Kingdom Weekend program has proven to be a most effective way to launch the studies by calling the Church to financial faithfulness.

On Saturday, training is held for a group of individuals selected and approved by their church to lead the Crown Financial Ministries Small Group Study. On Sunday, Buck calls the church to financial faithfulness in the morning service, with an optional afternoon or evening session. The opportunity is presented to the congregation to register to be part of the small groups that will be held at the church, commencing within a few weeks of the special weekend programs.

Recent comments from pastors about the weekend:

*"The seeds planted have taken root and **the Lord is using what you left behind.**"..."It is **one of the most valuable things** we have ever done here at the Chapel."..."It was **a very positive experience** for our fellowship to have you and your family here to minister."..."It has been **an experience that has turned this ministry around.**"..."Buck is a dynamic and motivating speaker...**hold onto your hats** when he gets up!"*

To God belongs all the glory!

For More Information on how you can develop a financial ministry at your church, contact: Advancing the Kingdom Ministries, 315-424-6180 or by email at atkm@atkministries.org

Visit us online at www.atkministries.org